O9-BHJ-995

We travel not for trafficking alone:
By hotter winds our fiery hearts are fanned:
For lust of knowing what should not be known
We make the Golden Journey to Samarkand.

JAMES ELROY FLECKER

A JOURNEY
TO
SAMARKAND

BY

LARRY WILLS HENDERSON

PUBLISHED BY

LONGMANS

GREEN

AND

COMPANY

In memory of

EDITH WILLS HENDERSON

who wanted me

to make this journey

CONTENTS

AUTHOR'S NOTE

This is the factual account of a journey in the Soviet Union. For the protection of certain individuals, some names of persons and places have been changed and the sequence of events occasionally altered. All the events narrated actually happened, however, and all conversations are reported verbatim.

AN ALBUM OF PHOTOGRAPHS
by Larry Henderson and Fred Peel

On a street in old Samarkand.

ABOVE, *A Moscow street.*
BELOW TOP, *For first class passengers—a private pool. At Yalta.*
BELOW BOTTOM, *With Mme Udolskaya in Alma-Ata.*
BELOW RIGHT, *The Mufti of Tashkent.*

ABOVE, *Most farms are still unmechanized. A collective near Odessa.*
BELOW LEFT, *Now closed, the "Church-on-Blood", Leningrad.*
BELOW RIGHT, *With the Metropolitan Nikolai (and translator), Moscow.*

ABOVE, *The Metallurgists' Sanatorium in Sochi cost $6 million to build.*
BELOW LEFT, *A lemon tree grew overnight. The Vorontzov Villa, Yalta.*
BELOW RIGHT, *Uzbek woman feeding her baby, Samarkand.*

1. *For Communists only. The Kharkov Hotel, Kharkov.*
2. *Where the Canadians stayed in Kharkov.*
3. *Eggs: 15c. a piece. The market place in Tbilisi.*

1. *Brickmakers in Samarkand.*
2. *Little children are taught to love Lenin. A youth camp.*
3. *The Golden Mosque Madresseh, Samarkand.*

1

2

3

ABOVE LEFT, *"Balconies a Romeo might climb"* in Tbilisi.
ABOVE RIGHT, *The Stalin Cotton Mill, Tashkent.*
BELOW, *Detail of brickwork from the Palace of Bibi Khanum, Samarkand.*

Gateway to the tomb of Tamerlane, Samarkand.

Shah-i-Zinda, the street of tombs, Samarkand.

FOREWORD

Why to Samarkand?
approaching the Soviet world; a visit to Moscow in 1957;
an interview with the Soviet Minister of Higher Education;
backstage at the Bolshoi;
I am invited to Soviet Central Asia; a tour is organized;
last-minute delay

When I told people that I was going to Samarkand, so many enquired where this was, what clothing I would require—furs or tropicals—whether I would travel by jet or by camel, that perhaps a word of explanation is necessary.

Samarkand was once the Capital of the Earth. True, a few unimportant and remote principalities escaped its suzerainty: England, France, the Papal See, the Holy Roman Empire, the Celestial Empire (China), the Hottentots and the Penguins. The vast territories of the New World had not yet been discovered.

But in the year of Our Lord 1400, all the world that was known and that mattered paid tribute to "the most illustrious and merciful monarch, the most great Sultan, the most mighty Warrior, the Lord Timur, Conqueror of the Earth." So runs the inscription over the door of the antechamber of Tamerlane's tomb in Samarkand.

Timur's capital was a mysterious blue city, encrusted with jewels, glittering under a burning sun like a sword, out on the deserts of Central Asia. So far did it lie beyond the ken of men and the means of travel, that to many it was a dream city, like Xanadu, or the New Jerusalem.

And so it remained. With the fall of Timur's empire, Samarkand disappeared behind the veil of history, time and distance. Overrun by warring tribes and later by the encroachments of the Russian Empire, the centre of Timurid glory literally vanished from human knowledge.

Central Asia became a forbidden area. The Imperial Russian governors, suspicious of foreign agents, refused visas to all but a few travellers.

An exception was Lord Curzon, who visited Samarkand in 1889. He wrote:

> Gladly would I expatiate upon [its] beauty, but it is more relevant to point out that, beyond having patched up the most glaring traces of dilapidation and made a few attempts, with deplorable results, to replace destroyed ornaments, the Russians have done nothing and are doing nothing whatever to preserve these sacred relics either from wanton demolition or from natural decay; and that, what with the depredations of vandals, the shock of earthquakes, and the lapse of time, the visitor of the twentieth century may find cause to enquire with resentful surprise what has become of the fabled grandeur of old Samarkand.

After this nineteenth-century glimpse, the curtain descended again. The Soviet Government, for reasons of its own, proved even more secretive than its czarist predecessor about its Asian dependencies. Travel to this area was strictly forbidden and visas were impossible to obtain. An occasional adventurer, like the intrepid Fitzroy Maclean, slipped through the loop-holes and brought back smuggled reports from old Samarkand. In 1949, in his book called *Eastern Approaches*, he reported:

> In character the old town had remained practically unchanged by the Russian invasion of 1868. Few Russians were to be seen in the streets. . . . Life seemed easy and

the inhabitants seemed to spend most of the time talking
and drinking tea out of shallow bowls in the innumerable
chai-khanas.

But is is only a question of time before all that remains
of a bygone civilization is swept away. Chancing to look
into the courtyard of a house in the old town, I was
not surprised to see some twenty little Uzbek girls of
three or four years old being marched briskly up and
down in fours and made to sing hymns to the glorious
Leader of the People.

Following in the footsteps of these indefatigable travellers, I
was determined to accomplish the journey for a dual purpose:
to write this book, and to make a colour-and-sound film of the
fabled blue city "half as old as time". This last—the film portion of my plan—would require official permission, as it was
most unlikely that I could slip through the cordon of the Soviet
secret police with three hundred and eighty pounds of sound-
film equipment!

Although I made out innumerable applications to the Soviet
Government (eight copies, in Russian, accompanied by a
lengthy autobiography for the files of the secret police), no
permit was forthcoming. Finally, I decided to apply to the pro-
per authorities in person. My opportunity came when I was
promised a visa to visit Moscow in June, 1957. The visa was to
be delivered at the Soviet Embassy in Warsaw, provided the
Soviet authorities approved.

The approaches to the Soviet world are sealed. It is not gen-
erally realized that the "iron curtain" is no mere rhetorical
phrase. It is a sealed area, stretching from the Baltic Sea to the
Black Sea, anything from five hundred yards to several miles
wide, defended by barbed wire and watchtowers and patrolled
by the Red Army. No one can get through, going either way,
without the express permission of the Soviet Government.

There are, however, some loop-holes. One of them is the

occupied city of Berlin. Reporting from Berlin in 1957, I contrasted the character of these two worlds, the Western and the Soviet, as they appeared side by side in this divided city:

> In the Potsdamer Platz, where East meets West, across a few yards of pavement, the contrast beween the two is brought sharply into focus.
>
> On the one side: the gay sidewalk cafés, the bright lights of department stores, well stocked with all the commodities of Western life, the giant pylons supporting the *Frei Berliner Presse*—the news of the world in moving lights. On the other side: the drab, grey, pot-holed streets, the State-owned H.O. Stores, with little on display and less available, the loud-speakers at the street corners, blaring forth the ceaseless propaganda:
>
>> "The Party is always right.
>> By Lenin established,
>> By Stalin confirmed,
>> The Party is always right."

It was not possible to cross the Iron Curtain at Berlin, however, because Canada does not recognize the East German Government and a transit visa could not be obtained. Instead, I travelled southward to Vienna, where, along with my cameraman Bob Crone, I boarded a Polish Airlines plane bound for Warsaw.

I entered the Communist world, therefore, through the gateway of the Polish Peoples' Democratic Republic. Here again, I remarked the same drastic drop in the standard of living. Warsaw, almost wholly destroyed in the Second World War, was still living amid ruins and desolation.

But the Poles are a vital and spirited people. Outwardly, their form of government might be Communist. But all the people I met, from newspaper editors to taxi-drivers, assured me that their sympathies were with the West. "You must not forget our geographical position," they said, referring obliquely

to the twenty-two Soviet divisions stationed between them and
the West.

Already I had begun to see that there were deep fissures in the
Communist world and that it was by no means the monolithic
structure it has been represented.

At the Soviet Embassy in Warsaw our Soviet visas were await-
ing us; and, after a short flight in a Soviet Aeroflot plane, we
landed at Moscow.

My initial reception was not promising. Soviet customs officers opened my bags and picked out a file of newspaper cut-
tings, containing my reports in the Toronto Daily Star. Un-
luckily, they opened it backwards, and began reading the re-
verse sides of all the pages—sports scores, the agony column,
help wanted, etc. Obviously suspicious stuff!

After making full notes on all this material, they kept me in
a waiting room for several hours until a senior official in the
uniform of the secret police, who creaked as he walked, as
though he wore stays, arrived. In a moment the atmosphere
changed. But of course I could enter the Soviet Union. I
offered to leave the incriminating documents in bond at the
airport, also all our sound-film equipment, but this suggestion
was brushed aside as unnecessary. "Please bring your equipment and be welcome!" said the security officer with a smile.

Evidently, I had been approved. This was even more apparent when, the following morning, an unexpected visitor called
on me at my hotel. He was Mr. Alexander Alexandrov, chief
political commentator at Moscow Radio. An affable, middle-
aged man of the Maxim Litvinov type, he had an excellent command of English and of the Western way of looking at things.

As always when newsmen get together, we began talking
shop. Alexandrov argued Russia's position with great ability.
His argument briefly: "Here we are. You are capitalists. We
are Communists. You are not going to change us, and we are
not going to change you. Let's co-exist."

Better still, he picked up the phone and set Moscow spinning
like a top for me—ministerial interviews, a visit backstage at
the Bolshoi, and many high-level contacts. I did not understand
this unexpected friendliness, but I was determined to take full
advantage of it.

One of my first interviews was with Mr. Viacheslav Elutin,
Soviet Minister of Higher Education. The Ministry was in a
bare old stone building, with a general air of dilapidation and
untidiness about it. But I was ushered through the green baize
doors of the Minister's office at exactly the hour of my appointment.

The Minister greeted me warmly, coming around his desk
and sitting beside me at a long conference table. We discussed
the implications of Soviet education, the emphasis on political
indoctrination, specialization in science, the export of experts
to under-developed countries.

It seemed apparent that the men in the Kremlin *believe* in
their leadership and in their goal and they no longer fear comparison with Western standards and techniques. "Tell your
people," said Minister Elutin, "that we welcome more ex-
changes with Western reporters, students, scientists and professional people of all kinds. Take them our greetings."

I seized upon his remark regarding reporters to make mention of my interest in Soviet Central Asia and my long-cher-
ished desire one day to see Samarkand. The Minister showed a
friendly and benevolent interest in this plan. "And why not?"
he said optimistically. I began to hope.

Throughout the remainder of my visit, this fair weather held.
We made films at the University, the theatre and the Bolshoi
Ballet. A special rehearsal was called at the Bolshoi for the
purpose. The stars of the season were not appearing at the time,
but several met me in one of the rehearsal rooms, so that we
might make films of the new ballet *Spartacus*, scheduled for its
performance in the fall of 1957.

Here was Maia Plissetskaia, the shapely blonde ballerina,
and Raisa Strouchkova, her dark and beautiful rival for the
mantle of the great Ulanova, who was in semi-retirement.

Here, too, was Aram Khachaturian, the composer, and Alexander Lapaury, who stages the ballets at the Bolshoi.

What I saw was a ballet actually in the process of creation, as the stars worked it out, under the guidance of the composer and the choreographer. The atmosphere was friendly and informal. We sat on benches around the mirror-lined room and watched the principals and their partners go through the *pas de deux*. Between work-outs, I asked the questions that were uppermost in my mind.

What is the chief difference between Soviet and Western ballet? According to Lapaury, Western ballet is based on *divertissement* form, whereas Soviet ballets are whole works with a central plot (and socialist moral). This makes longer roles for the principals and consequently harder work. Mlle Plissetskaia joined in. "Yes," she said, "to dance a Soviet ballet is the equivalent of a track and field star breaking a world record every evening!"

What is the life of a ballet artist under State control? Petite Mlle Strouchkova answered me. At the age of nine she was taken by her parents, who had noted her talent for dancing, before a State examining board. Thereafter her education was designed with one objective: to produce a ballet star. Living at home, but trained at State expense, Raisa went to ballet school every day. In the summertime she was sent to a camp for a month's rest. By the time she finished school (at eighteen) she was taken on as a soloist at the Bolshoi.

How much money can a Soviet artist make? Mlle Strouchkova smiled at me reprovingly. "Soviet artists do not look upon their work as a means of making money," she said. "Their every need is taken care of by the State. The State buys my slippers and tights. The State pays for cleaning my costumes. I do not even have to save for my retirement, as the State gives me a pension for life. As a result, Soviet artists are completely free to give themselves over to the art of creation. It is only under these conditions," concluded the charming ballerina, "that the high standards of Soviet art are possible."

Moscow smiled on me, and I smiled back. In many interviews like the foregoing, I heard arguments for the constructive side of Soviet life. And, indeed, constructiveness seemed the operative word to describe the Soviet scene. Everywhere I looked, from my special Intourist limousine, I saw construction projects; there seemed to be so much traffic on the streets, so many attractions at the ballet, the theatre, and the circus, that it certainly looked like the hub of a great world.

But never did I succeed in getting behind the façade. All the people I spoke to were Communist officials or professional servants of the régime. Among students at the University I tried to strike up a conversation. Our exchange was brief and formal, conducted by an official interpreter. At the theatre I tried to exchange some remarks with members of the audience, but my neighbours either had, or feigned to have, no knowledge of English. People in the streets and parks seemed to draw away from me when I approached them. I was told that to visit a Russian home without an introduction (*i.e.* from a government source) would be an inadmissible invasion of privacy.

Before I left, Mr. Alexandrov came to me with an invitation to visit Soviet Central Asia as a guest of the Soviet Government. It seemed too good to be true! But I had other commitments that required my immediate return to Canada. I promised to write Mr. Alexandrov as soon as the trip could be arranged and to return to the Soviet Union. We shook hands warmly and parted.

It was two years before my dream was realized. But by then many things had happened. I wrote Mr. Alexandrov of my plan, but my letter went unanswered. On the other hand, the Soviet Union was rapidly opening up to foreign travel. Among the cities put on the open list was Samarkand.

I applied, therefore, through the Soviet Embassy in Ottawa for visas for myself and my camera-man—this time, Glenn Platt. At the same time, I had determined that any visit to the Soviet Union was valueless that did not penetrate the façade.

For this purpose, I needed associates who could speak Russian. So I advertised a tour of the Soviet Union for thirty days, leaving New York on June 30th, 1959. The tour was organized for me by Air France, one of the few air-lines to fly directly into Moscow.

For months I pored over maps, trying to work out an itinerary that would include as many places, as far off the beaten path, as possible. This time, I wanted to see the *real* Russia. A list of towns and cities open to foreign travel was supplied to me by the Soviet Intourist organization, but I found that the inclusion of too many out-of-the way places was not acceptable to them. Neither did they favour too long a stay in many of the more remote and inaccessible places.

At last the following itinerary was agreed upon: Moscow—Leningrad—Kiev—Odessa—Yalta—Sochi—Tbilisi—Kharkov—Moscow. This was the public part of the tour, to be completed in thirty days. The remainder of the journey to Alma-Ata, Tashkent, and Samarkand was to be completed in fourteen days by myself and my camera-man alone.

I was fortunate in my travelling companions. They were eighteen Canadians, including four young women, from all parts of the country, and representing many different professions, such as medicine, dentistry, law, transport, manufacturing, and civic government. More important still, I secured the inclusion of three Russian and Ukrainian-speaking members, and one of Estonian origin. With the help of these, I hoped to be able to make genuine contact with the Soviet people and to explore the country at the unofficial level.

Seven days before my departure, all visa formalities had been completed for my group, even for those of Russian extraction, which involved lengthy examination. But my own passport had not been returned by the Soviet Embassy in Ottawa. A telephone enquiry revealed the appealing fact that "it has not been found possible to grant Mr. Henderson a visa."

More consultation by phone. The Ambassador's secretary

was unable to give any reason for the refusal. He was very polite, but "these matters are up to Moscow." I pointed out that my intention to visit the Soviet Union had been known to them for five months. He promised to refer the matter back to Moscow.

Next day I flew to Ottawa from my home in Toronto. I presented myself at the Soviet Embassy, a grey, cheerless-looking building on Charlotte Street. I waited for more than an hour in a reception room, furnished with red plush chairs, tables covered with fringed rugs, and stuffed birds on the mantlepiece.

At last the Consul, Mr. Selivanov, accompanied by the Ambassador's secretary, came in to see me. I could guess nothing from their faces. But the Consul handed me my passport. Looking inside, I saw that it contained a visa for the Soviet Union.

No explanation for the abrupt reversal of policy was given. However, Mr. Selivanov did invite me genially to sit down for a chat. Careful to preface his remarks by saying that he was not trying to dictate what I should write about the Soviet Union, the Consul nevertheless adjured me to "look for the best" and to avoid "criminal elements".

"Try to catch the spirit of enthusiasm in our people," he said. The Russia he described to me was an exciting and promising world. I got the impression that he really thought and felt about his homeland in this way.

He also gave me his personal assurance that, although I was travelling on a tourist visa, I would be "free to report as a newsman" for press and television.

I went to the Soviet Union with the intention of looking for everything and reporting everything. It is not possible, at best, to catch more than a fragmentary glimpse of this mysterious and often contradictory country. The more we know about it, how its people live and think and feel, the better we may judge what its future will be.

I hope the fragments of information, glimpses and impressions I have gathered here may help to build a picture of the Soviet world. It is not, let me hasten to say, the whole picture and it will not please everyone. But it is mine.

CHAPTER

1

MOSCOW KALEIDOSCOPE

Arrival in Moscow;
the Ukraine Hotel; Tamara, our Soviet guide;
the façade: boulevards, university, agricultural exhibition;
the reality: back streets, farmers' market,
Baptist church, Kommission stores, black market,
stilyagi, Gorki Park

"Mockba." The Russian letters in red over the airport still spelt mystery. My heart was pounding as I crossed the tarmac to the terminal building. Everywhere, the uncommunicative Russian faces—the incomprehensible language—the queer looking-glass writing. Would I ever break through these barriers and discover the real Russia?

The real Russia. That's what I came to find. I was afraid of it; I was fascinated by it. How little I dreamed, at that moment, that Russia itself was waiting, just as eagerly as I, to open its secrets! But that came later—after I had learned the sign-language and the passwords.

For the moment, I just consulted my phrase-book and then addressed a blonde young lady in a red dress. "*Izvenetia, paja-lousta, gdye Intourist?*"

"You must be Mr. Henderson," she said with a smile. "Welcome to Russia!"

Within a few moments, I knew that her name was Tamara,

she was the Intourist guide assigned to my group, and she had a bus ready and waiting to take us to our hotel. I felt better already.

The Russia Tamara showed me is Communist Russia. It is not the only Russia, and its claim to represent the Russian people I found to be quite wrong. But it is there. It is a façade of gigantic proportions, sometimes noble, sometimes false, but inescapable.

No escape was possible, for example, from the Intourist hotel in which we were lodged. The Ukraine Hotel is a monolithic monstrosity, such as Genghis Khan himself might have dreamed up under the influence of hashish. Thirty stories high, it is cleverly designed to look higher, by means of an optical-trick spire and several tons of ornamental masonry in the form of gigantic urns, pineapples and palm fronds around the towers.

Escape was impossible for two reasons. First, all arrangements for accommodation in the Soviet Union are made by Intourist, the government organization in charge of foreigners. Intourist—not the tourist—chooses the hotel. Second, there is no stairway in the Ukraine. One thousand rooms are served by elevator alone, at irregular and infrequent intervals. In the event of fire, power failure or sheer hunger, the only escape is by jumping in the Moskva River!

The hub of every hotel in the Soviet Union is the Intourist office. Opening off the bare marble foyer, the one at the Ukraine is a sort of parlour, completely furnished in red plush, a-buzz with activity. Behind a row of desks, respectively labelled "Air travel", "Limousines", "Theatre tickets", tired-looking Intourist officials try to cope with the barrage of questions and demands.

The first morning after our arrival, I sat down in a corner of the Intourist office with our interpreter, Tamara. Our group included a number of specialists, and I wanted to make arrangements for them to see the things in which they were interested.

"But that is impossible!" Tamara was speaking. Crisply, firmly, shaking her young blonde head, she laid down the law.

"A group is a group. They must stay together. They must do the same things, eat the same things, stay in the same place. You must rule them with an iron hand."

I looked at this young lady with a new interest. She was extremely attractive, in a North American way. Unlike all the other Intourist girls, with their round, stolid features, hair in a bun and high-necked dresses, Tamara was different. She wore her hair in a page-boy bob, with a water wave. Her lips were painted scarlet to match her nails. Her red dress, although home-made, was cut in Western style to show her slender figure to best advantage. I began to wonder what we had done to deserve Tamara!

Yet there she was, talking like part of the machine — which of course she was. Her job was to "interpret" for the group, but also to supervise our activities, order our meals in advance, book our hotels, trains, planes and cars, and make sure that we did not exceed our daily budget (which was paid in advance). It seemed a tall order for a slight, pretty girl, especially such a young one.

To break the ice, therefore, I presented Tamara with an enamelled pin, in the shape of a maple-leaf. Although Soviet women wear no jewellery, Tamara promptly pinned it on her dress. She wore it throughout most of the journey. Then I spoke up.

"Tamara," I said, "I think you will find that Canadians cannot be ruled with an iron hand. It is best to try the velvet glove."

"We'll see!" she said gaily, tossing back her golden hair. And she began making out our programme—her way.

Moscow is a barbaric capital. On a morning walk through these wide boulevards, that was my first thought. They are impossibly wide, these boulevards, ten or twelve lanes across, without any islands. The cars and trucks come charging down, without the least slackening of pace, as they scatter pedestrians wildly like pigeons.

Down the centre of the boulevard is a middle lane, marked

by two white lines. No ordinary car ever uses this lane, nor does any pedestrian, even in the utmost extremity, take refuge there. I was told it is a "privilege" lane for the men in black limousines.

There is something barbarous about these stone-faced buildings, too, modern as they are. Perhaps it is the lack of any civilized appendages: the windows are without shutters or awnings, the entrances have no brass door handles, knockers, welcome mats, railings, or letter boxes. They have a closed look, these buildings; they are fortresses.

People throng the streets, moving slowly in great herds, without any urgent sense of destination. They have an animal ease and vitality; the men dress with arrogant carelessness, the women without any trace of style, although many are pretty. But there is no sense of personality, of differentation. I wondered about their lives—what kind of houses they have—if they are happy, and if so, why they do not smile. But all that lies on the other side of the façade. . . .

There are seven skyscrapers in Moscow altogether—all built in the same style. One is the University, of which Muscovites are inordinately proud. Its Mongoloid silhouette, supporting the elongated spire and red star, is reproduced on countless postcards, medals and souvenirs. I even saw a reproduction of it used as a stage setting for a play by Mayakovsky. So there is no getting away from it—the Russians like this kind of thing.

Passing through its portals, on my first morning in Moscow I entered the world that Communists like the best—the world of learning. Here the mind is shaped and moulded to fit the preconceived plan; the theory predominates over the actuality. I looked at the vast library, served by "the most efficient book delivery in the world", according to my guide. Books by the Marx-Engels school on the conditioning of the human species. Books by Lysenko on the inheritance of conditioned mutations in plants. Books by Pavlov on conditioned reflex in humans. Much of this literature is not accepted on a scientific basis in the outside world. But here, in these hushed precincts, it is the word of the Law.

Moscow University has about 23,000 students, of which nearly half are housed under this one roof. They come from all over the world, from China, India, the United Arab Republic, France, England and Canada, to drink at the fountain of Marxist knowledge. Ten per cent of the curriculum is compulsory Marxism: dialectical materialism, historical materialism, and history of the Communist Party.

I stopped two Russian girls in a corridor, each carrying heavy bags. I offered to help, but they laughingly refused. The bags were full of stones. Geology students. They showed me their living-quarters, two neat adjoining rooms on the thirty-second floor, with central hall between—rent, two dollars a month. Money was no problem to them. They were both paid salaries while studying of thirty dollars a month as first-year students, rising to fifty dollars in their fifth year.

Before leaving, I asked the girls if they would like to know anything about Canada and our educational system. I invited them to ask questions. "No need," intervened the interpreter efficiently. "They already know everything about Canada— geography, history, literature and class struggle. They do not need to ask questions!" Rather wistfully, I thought, the girls said good-bye.

I wanted to see how people lived. Accordingly, a visit to the new workers' flats was arranged by the Intourist agency. This new residential area, on the road to the airport, stretches for five continuous miles, flanked on both sides by bare, stone-faced buildings, five to eight stories high, all exactly alike.

There community apartments, including shops, nursery, schools, and department stores, are much admired, especially for the speed and method of their construction. The latter appears imaginative and hazardous in the extreme. Everything is done by pre-fabrication; ceilings, floors, staircases, whole walls including window-frames, are wheeled into place by gantry cranes. An entire block for two hundred people is put up in four months, by two crews of seventeen men, each working eight-hour shifts. This is three or four times the productivity per worker in the West, and illustrates admirably the Russian flair for the spectacular.

On closer examination, however, many of the finished details seem shoddy. Bathroom tiles, balconies, even the stone facing, often appear to be falling apart only a year after construction. In one case, I noted an inlaid wooden floor that was missing several pieces, even before the remainder of the building was up.

All this construction, of course, is undertaken by Government agencies—Gostroy, the Council of Ministers of Construction, and Gosplan, the State Planning Commission—since every building and the land on which it stands belongs to the Government.

As a landlord the Government appears quixotically generous. Rent is less than 10 per cent of a worker's average earnings and would hardly seem to justify the expense of the housing scheme. But then the Government can take it out of his income in other ways, by vastly underpaying him for his labour, since all salaries are set by the Government too.

What fun they must have, the Masters of Everything, counting the money and planning how to spend it as they please! And if they put up five miles of workers' flats and forget to install a single fire-escape—well, who is going to complain? The Masters of Everything decide who is going to live in them, too.

If sheer size were the measure of all things, I suppose the Moscow Agricultural Exhibition would be the greatest show on earth. At any rate, it is certainly the crown of the façade, the grand climax in the illusionist spectacle. After this, the spectator is sent away stupefied by the grandeur of it all.

On a Sunday morning, Russian families turn up by thousands, carrying rugs and picnic baskets. People from all parts of the Soviet Union—many in unique national dress—add gaiety and worldliness to the crowd. For this is how Soviet citizens are encouraged to live—in public, under the stimulus of group conditioning. It is the full flower of collectivist civilization.

Along the red walks of crushed brick, myriads of roses bloom —every one a "peace" rose. The loud-speakers attached to the lamp-posts play cultural music, interspersed with "news" of national importance: industrial targets surpassed, agricultural quotas over-fulfilled, scientific records broken. The world on this Sunday morning seems wonderfully serene and inspirational.

Let us stop before the great fountain girt with golden maidens, representing the sheave-gatherers, with its central cascade of water greater in volume and noise than anything imaginable. (When I ask direction to a drinking-fountain, however, I am told there is none in the park.) Before us stretches the panorama of the exhibit: two miles of pavilions, glittering in gold and mosaic, each representing the style of the individual republics of the Soviet Union.

One of the first is the Karelian Pavilion, built of sturdy logs, with a frieze of wood-carving, representing the struggle for independence of these northern woodsmen. (It is closed, unfortunately, since the Karelian-Finnish Republic has now been absorbed into the Russian Republic.) At the Uzbek Pavilion, glowing in blue tile, I catch my first glimpse of the glory of Samarkand. Inside, however, I find no further hint of the magic city—only displays of Russian tractors, Russian turbines, and Russian heavy industrial equipment. It is the same at the Kazakh Pavilion, the Ukrainian Pavilion, and the Georgian Pavilion. The exteriors are truly national, but the interiors are all Russian. (Does this thought trouble any of the nationals from each republic as they stroll through their own exhibits?)

The atomic reactor dazzles the crowd. They gawk at the mechanical hands that operate the controls inside the radioactive glass chamber. They shudder a little with awe before the unearthly blue flame that glows over the tank of heavy water — the visible manifestation of atomic power generated before their

eyes. In the background, a loud-speaker is blaring in Russian.
The words, translated to me by a member of my group, are:
"While the United States of America spent $83 million last
year on building new prisons for its people, the Soviet Union
spent this sum on building atomic projects for the good of all
mankind."

All this is Moscow—yet not the Moscow I came to see. My
Moscow is another city, not in the least pretentious, non-political, human—the Moscow behind the façade. It is not hard to
find, although it is not included in the official tour. Just stop at
the first *pereolok*, or lane leading off one of the main boulevards.
Turn into it. Right away, you are in the other Moscow.

The *pereolok* is narrow. Probably there is no sidewalk, but
the cobblestones are spotlessly clean, scrubbed and washed by
a legion of women with pails and brooms. The buildings are of
wood, not stone—large, heavy logs, caulked together, the
windows prettily decorated with wooden fretwork on the gables.
Glimpsed through these windows are tiny rooms, each one an
individual home, with two or three beds, stoves and chimney
pipes, wooden chairs and tables, wardrobes, sometimes even a
television set! This is how by far the greater number of citizens
live—not in the modern showplaces reserved for the party
hacks.

Here and there is a courtyard behind an archway. In the centre is an old hand pump; the date on it may be of the last
century. Women are filling pails, chatting and nodding; some
men are building a shed for wood to burn in the winter. In the
corner of the yard a man lies curled up, ignored by all even at
midday. An empty vodka bottle peers out of his pocket. A
bearded priest, in black robes emblazoned by a gold cross,
brushes past, perhaps on an errand of mercy.

A little farther on, there is a small square, filled with covered
stalls, where the farmers come to sell the produce of their own
private plots. Anything worth the eating is to be found here, so

the square is a-buzz. But what prices! Cabbages, a dollar apiece. Onions, forty cents a pound. Eggs, fifteen cents each. A chicken that weighs on the scales at two and a half pounds, $5.50— more than two days' pay for an average working man. Most people buy meat in milligrams.

My friend and companion, Israel Ginsburg, who speaks Russian fluently, had the following encounter in the market. A young woman, noting his Western dress and supposing him to be a person of influence, plucked his sleeve. *"Mir, pajalousta!* (Peace, please!)"* As though this power lay in his hand! Israel was deeply moved.

"What shall I say to you?" he said. "We belong to different worlds. I believe in God. You do not."

All at once the farmers set up a shout: "We *do* believe! We believe!"

I was astonished and doubtful. Religion is still officially condemned in Russia. Then a visiting Australian minister gave me the address of a Baptist Church in Moscow. The following Sunday, I attended service. A small building, built on the lines of a Congregational Church, it was filled to overflowing. A thousand jammed the galleries and floor, and as many more stood in the corridors and in the street outside.

The bearded pastor preached an hour-long sermon on a text from St. Luke: "And I say unto you, Ask, and it shall be given you; seek, and ye shall find; knock, and it shall be opened unto you." Men and women, young and old, in about equal proportions, listened with evangelical fervour and wiped away many tears. Afterwards I told the minister, the Rev. Mr. Jacob Zhidkov, that the members of his congregation were not the only ones who wept. Many in my group did the same.

His church, he said, has 4,500 members and there are Baptist churches in 5,300 communities in the Soviet Union. He spoke in simple, positive terms. "We are preaching the Gospel everywhere in our country," he said. "We hope for success. God is omnipotent and He is with us."

Shopping in the *pereolok* is very different from along the big boulevards. Of course, the Government owns all the stores in the city and sets all the prices. In the big stores, only new government products are sold. In the back streets, however, much of the business is done by the commission shops. These are really pawn-shops, in which you may find the most unlikely articles, none of which ever came from a government-owned factory.

Here I can spend a whole afternoon, picking over antique samovars, eighteenth-century miniatures, vodka cups in old pewter, Diana hunting in bronze, hand-painted china Easter eggs inscribed with the letters XB, meaning Christ Arisen. Again the prices are high and again I hear the argument that anything worth buying is exceptionally dear in Moscow. Consumer goods of quality are in extremely short supply.

Not all aspects of back-street shopping in Moscow are savoury. There is a brisk trade in a number of illicit goods. Bicycle tires, car parts, even lighters are sold from under the counters. This is a grey market. Then there are black-market items like American jazz records, nylons, and books in English. They will buy your clothes, your shoes, your ball-point pen. Hottest item of all is money.

The official rate of exchange for tourists is ten roubles to the dollar. Standing in front of a well-known department store, with my passport in my hand, I was approached by a young man with an American sports shirt and a Russian accent, who said:

"You got any big bills?"

"How big?" I said warily.

"I give you twenty roubles to the dollar for $20 bills and thirty roubles to the dollar for $50 bills."

Who buys these bills from the black-marketeer would be interesting to know.

The Praga Restaurant is a haunt for the young renegades of Communist society. It is also a very expensive restaurant, which leads to some interesting questions. How do some people in the

Soviet Union acquire their money? Why do the children of such people cut themselves adrift from conventional collectivist ideas? As capital grows, what will become of Communism?

The crowd at the Praga is dressed in the uniform of their clique. The boys wear their hair long and affect American clothes, with very narrow black trousers and black shirts or turtleneck sweaters; the girls wear cropped hair and tight-fitting blouses and skirts. These are the *stilyagi* or style-chasers— sons and daughters of the well-to-do, who have nothing to spend their money on, for pleasures in Soviet society are strictly limited to conformist entertainment.

So they gather at the Praga and talk, make love and get very drunk. Champagne corks pop, glasses are smashed and voices are raised. A girl sings sentimentally:

Three coins in the fountain. . . each one seeking happiness. . .

On summer evenings, young people of the working class take to the parks. At the landing stages along the Moskva River, they line up for places on the motor launch. The fare to Gorki Park is eighteen cents. It is cool and bright in the long twilight of these midsummer nights. The young couples sit, arms enlaced—clean, healthy boys, girls without a trace of make-up.

At Gorki Park station everyone files off quietly. The clown who jumps from the rail of the boat to the dock is severely scolded by the woman ticket-collector. From the bank comes the sound of a dance band among the trees. In a clearing, a crowd of perhaps five thousand are dancing on the bare earth to the music of a six-piece band. The music is staid and conventional—the dancing is not. Boogie-woogie, rock 'n roll, they do it all.

On the fringes of the crowd, small groups collect, playing impromptu games. A young man turns his back on the crowd, crosses his arms, places one hand behind his ear, palm outward. A girl comes up behind him and hits his palm with hers as hard as possible. He turns and guesses who it was. If he guesses right, he has won and the girl takes his place. The crowd screams with delight and the game goes on.

Others stand in queues for a turn on the ferris wheel, or on the giant swings, that travel upward in an arc fifty feet high. One terrifying stunt is the "human hammer". A man sits astride a sort of spring-board, which swings him up through the air and brings him down head first, inches from the concrete floor, before it stops, reverses itself, and swings him back again. Nerves of steel these people have.

Under the overhanging trees, on the grassy banks far from the band and the ice-cream parlours and the midway — other games are going on. There are quiet whisperings and soft laughter among the shadows.

This is the real Moscow behind the façade. It is a world to itself, infinite in its variety, impervious to conformity, Russian rather than Communist. This is how the people of this great city of nearly seven million really live: mostly in poverty, but with great dignity, resourcefulness and humanity.

This was the Russia I longed to know.

CHAPTER

2

THROUGH THE LOOKING-GLASS

Upside down and inside out—the technique of Communism;
the propaganda machine;
the religion of Lenin;
the spy system; why trust nobody?; the watchbirds;
Mme Ivanova and the Committee for Cultural Relations

Those who cherish a belief that Communism is just another way of life, perhaps not too dissimilar to our own, are apt to be bewildered at first in the Soviet Union. The first impression seems to be that *everything* is different, or opposite to what we expect, not only in basic concepts, but also in the most trivial detail. It is as though we had, indeed, passed through Alice's looking-glass into a country where everything is wrong-side round.

An example that sticks in my mind occurred before we even disembarked at Moscow airport. Besides the Western tourists aboard, the passenger list included a Soviet delegation returning home from abroad. As the door of the plane was opened, the Soviet group was called out first, while the remainder of us were advised to remain in our seats. There was a presentation of flowers at the foot of the gangway, speeches were made, photos were taken. Only after all the formalities of the Soviet homecoming were over were the Westerners, sweltering in their seats, allowed to disembark. In any civilized country of the world, I think, the ordinary passengers would have been allowed off first and the delegation last.

This inversion of what we regard as normal runs like a thread through the whole fabric of Soviet society. Here are people who are straining every resource to reach the moon, before they have solved most of the problems of everyday life. Soviet *sputniks* probe the uncharted reaches of interplanetary space before cars, refrigerators, or most ordinary appliances are placed within the reach of the average citizen.

Where we restrain undue public spending on such facilities as airports, parks, stadia, theatres, and legislatures, Soviet expenditure will be on the most lavish scale. Where we strive to raise the standard of home life, most Soviet families are living in a single room. While Soviet science astounds the world, the industrial heart of many a Communist enterprise is manufactured in the capitalist West. Even the twenty-one printing presses on which the chief organ of Communist propaganda, *Pravda*, is published were built and are maintained by Britons.

And, of course, the whole framework of popular beliefs is turned topsy-turvy, too. Concepts we consider good—a free press, free elections and free speech—are regarded by doctrinaire Communists quite differently. Long arguments on these matters only produce such strictures upon our way of thinking as this statement, made by one of my guides: "You Westerners are too conceited about freedom. There are other things more important than that. Social justice, for instance. Now take Little Rock. . . ."

One of the most dismaying revelations is the discrepancy that has grown up between what we and they take to be the accepted historical facts. Even non-political citizens of the Soviet Union seem persuaded, on the basis of much "factual" evidence, that South Korea invaded North Korea in June, 1950, not vice versa. A teacher of history in Tashkent told me that Russia won the Second World War single-handed, with entirely negligible assitance from Britain and the United States. The director of a large hospital in Sochi denied to me that Sir Alexander Fleming discovered penicillin. It was apparently a certain Professor Yermolnya of the Soviet Academy of Sciences.

How do we know what we know? Can any of us be sure that things really did happen the way we believe they did? Were we there? So begins the process called brain-washing. Black is no longer black. White is no longer white. It is whatever you choose to call it.

I never did have a discussion with a Communist in which I was able to establish any valid point. The game was always lost before it began, because the rules were changed. It is a salutary, if exasperating, experience. We all need to re-examine the basis of our thinking from time to time. But it is the first gambit in the technique of Communism.

Once the mind has been cut adrift from all established principles and points of reference, it is susceptible to the hypnotism of propaganda. The role of propaganda in modern life is of incalculable proportion in determining the tastes, desires and beliefs of the masses. In the Western world its influence is curbed, however, by the conflict of promoters. Only when the media of propaganda fall into the hands of a single individual or group is there an acute danger. In the Soviet world, of course, the control of the machinery of propaganda by the State is total.

It is only natural that this power over the minds of the Soviet people is used to promote faith in Communist principles and to suppress or counter any heretical beliefs. The extent of its dissemination, however, commands our awe. Not for an instant is the mind of the Soviet citizen allowed to drift without direction. As the political director of a trade union told me: "It is the duty of the State to educate the citizens during every hour of every day."

The machine itself is massive. Not only does it control the entire educational system but it operates in every place of assembly, employment or recreation. From one end to the other, the Soviet Union is wired with loud-speakers—along the main streets, in the parks, in hotels; there is literally no refuge from the voice of authority. The speakers carry cultural music, or exhortations to harder work, or sometimes the message may be "news"—such as the little item I heard one day concerning the tragic number of deaths by starvation in America. It seems seven thousand had died in one week in the state of Illinois. Many more had been picked up, the blood gushing from their ears—evidently a sign of extreme malnutrition.

The newspapers themselves are given over entirely to phantasies of this sort. The issues of *Pravda* or *Izvestia* (the latter run by Premier Khrushchov's son-in-law) are usually four-page editions in which only a few items of foreign news appear on page four. Canadian events may be represented by the summary of a speech by Tim Buck. Accidents on foreign air-lines, floods, or tornadoes account for the rest. Foreign political matters get practically no coverage. It is a curious fact that at the height of the Berlin crisis and the Geneva conference of 1959, I saw only the slightest mention of this grave international situation.

By contrast, all news of the Soviet scene is encouraging and uplifting. "Seven blast furnaces built in record time." I quote at random from a single copy of the English-language *Moscow News*. "New brilliant achievements of the Soviet Union in the exploration of cosmic space." "Rally of one thousand million builders of Communism." "Cellulose output to increase 50 per cent." "N. S. Khrushchov says that truthful, realistic art serves peace." Even the lessons in the "Russian [language] Corner" carry the same spirit of optimism, *e.g.* "The sky is clear . . . the girl is happy. . . the book is interesting." Tidings of comfort and joy.

No news of disaster or crime is ever reported in the Soviet Union — unless foreigners are involved. To judge by the papers, no accidents, earthquakes, murders, robberies or swindles ever take place. I was told by a young Russian worker in Leningrad, in the course of a private conversation, that a Soviet plane crashed in that city in August of 1958, killing or injuring four hundred people. Not a word of it ever appeared in the press. This Pollyanna type of reporting may seem commendable to some, in contrast to the kind of fare served up to Western readers. But it cannot pretend to be genuine news.

Visual propaganda is equally wide-spread, although hardly on the scale of American billboard advertising. It only seems more prevalent, because it promotes the wares of a single sponsor, the State. Citizens are exhorted to work harder, to fulfil the Seven-Year Plan, to help overtake America, to observe the rules of Socialist duty, to drink more milk, and to acquire culture. Some advertising mentions specific commodities, all State products, but oddly enough many of these are not apparently on the market as yet. In Sochi I observed the sign "Five hundred million pairs of shoes by 1965!" (Actually, since there are over two hundred million people in the Soviet Union, this works out at two and a half pairs in six years.)

In a more indirect form, the propaganda message assumes a crypto-religious character. Religion, of course, in the accepted sense, has been officially condemned. But no one can see the reverential treatment accorded the memory of Lenin without sensing its religious overtones. In every city square, park, museum, or hotel lobby stands "the founder of our Communist state", in heroic pose, arm extended like Moses coming down from Sinai with the tablets of the Law.

Every morning, long before the light breaks, the line forms in Red Square in Moscow before the red-granite mausoleum of Lenin and Stalin. Soon it is four thousand long, shuffling, docile, the men in the peaked caps and black cloth suits that denote country folk come to town; the women wearing those big head shawls they call babushkas, black stockings, and aprons.

The Veneration of the Tomb has inescapable echoes of the Holy Sepulchre. We descend a flight of stairs to a dim, clammy chamber, where the temperature is kept at thirty-five degrees F. Again we ascend, to the catafalque where the embalmed bodies lie. Here are no candles, but a strong red light playing on the faces of Lenin (in black serge suit) and Stalin (in grey marshal's uniform), flanked by the equally motionless, but living, forms of the young Red Army guard of honour.

The line of worshippers pauses before the body of Lenin, his face small and waxen, his hand no longer extended in authority. Is this the Saviour of the new faith? Communists deny such an inference hotly. But why then the worship of the relics, the embalment, the iconography? And is he not, too, proclaimed the Prince of Peace?

Propaganda provokes its own reaction. It invites criticism in direct proportion to the extravagance of its claims. If the Soviet were not a perfectionist society, which seeks to impose its formula on the whole world, one would not be tempted to expose its imperfections.

Propaganda is the positive face the Soviet state presents to us. Its negative face remains unseen, lurking behind the immense machinery of the secret police. The stories are legion concerning the operation of this most feared intelligence service in the world. One was told me by Dan Schorr, lately Moscow correspondent of the Columbia Broadcasting System. Most hotel rooms assigned to Western reporters are traditionally supposed to be wired with hidden microphones. Schorr located his in the air ventilator over the bed. One day, the correspondent of the *New York Times* was up in his room, bemoaning his luck. He had not been able to secure a single interview at the Kremlin. "I just can't get through to them," he moaned.

"Well, you're through to them now!" said Schorr. And he told him about the hidden microphone. Getting the idea, the *New York Times* man stood on the bed in front of the ventilator and sounded off his complaints. Ten minutes later, the phone rang. "Is the *New York Times* representative there? Well, this is the Press Office. We have arranged an interview for you tomorrow with Mr. Khrushchov!" You can't say that the system is inefficient! Just different, that's all.

Reporters and other Westerners who try to beat the system resort to written messages, even in the privacy of their rooms. The farce of carrying out such precautions is sometimes tedious and unbearable. On one occasion, my camera-man told me he did not believe the Russians had any microphones capable of picking up conversations from behind plaster walls or wooden floor-boards. He had spent an entire day in Moscow electrical shops trying to locate a microphone to replace his own, which had been damaged in transit. "They simply haven't got any high-grade equipment," he said.

Later on, I spent the evening with the attaché of a Western embassy at his flat in Moscow. He showed me the microphones, eight altogether, that he had found in the ceiling of his flat. They were tiny, extremely sensitive, and so finely built that they had no magnetic fields by which they could be detected. A crack in the ceiling near the light fixture had led to the discovery. "Don't let anyone tell you they can't make them," he said; "they're just not in the stores, that's all." After that, we went back to writing notes.

Conversations at Western embassies touching upon any private matter usually take place on an open balcony, or in the garden. No one is trusted, especially the Russian staff assigned to the Embassy. While riding in the back seat of an embassy car, I was discussing some interesting contacts I had made. My companion, a Western diplomat, silenced me, indicating the chauffeur, who wore the uniform and badge of a Western government. "One can't be too careful," he remarked.

This atmosphere of suspicion extends even to the nationals of Western powers. Westerners who come to the Soviet Union on student exchange or cultural missions are frequently induced to work for or with the Soviet Government. Many of them are university students, who may have had pro-Communist sympathies in the first place. Others become involved with Russian girls, and are persuaded to play a double game. Some are entrapped in compromising situations, and blackmailed into serving the Communist cause. No one can be trusted, even among one's fellow-countrymen, once we pass through into the looking-glass land.

One day I called at the home of the Canadian military attaché, Squadron Leader Sidney Mitchell. He and his wife, a charming couple, know and love Russia deeply. Mrs. Mitchell speaks Russian like a native and makes friends easily among ordinary people. The Squadron Leader is a powerful man with a fine personality.

Not long ago he was involved in a "diplomatic scandal", fabricated by Russian security forces. He was travelling on a train to Tbilisi with three other Western officers. *En route,* they were each assigned to separate compartments on the train. So with the co-operation of Russian fellow-passengers, they arranged to exchange seats so all four could be in one compartment. The "agent" in charge of the railway carriage appeared quite agreeable.

Later, however, the agent seemed to have received orders, for some reason, to break up the group. He insisted that each of the officers should return to his former place. This they refused to do. A Russian passenger boarded the train at a wayside station with a ticket for a berth in the Canadians' compartment. He refused to take a berth in any other compartment, and remained standing in the corridor all night. (Actually, says Mitchell, he was the "tail" assigned to follow them). Afterwards, *Komsomolskaya Pravda,* the organ of the Communist Youth movement, published an editorial denouncing the "hooliganism" of the Western officers, who, it was alleged, also wilfully damaged furnishings, tore light fixtures from the walls, and so on. This charge was reprinted in leading Canadian newspapers without comment. No mention was made of the fact that the allegations were never proved and were later withdrawn.

This is the kind of defamation that all Westerners risk who live in the Soviet Union. In this case, the object appeared to be to force the expulsion of certain foreign military personnel. In other cases, such charges are designed to show up Westerners in an unfavourable light, as crude and uncultured individuals, not to be trusted by peace-loving Soviet citizens.

Suspicion of Westerners is undoubtedly inculcated by the Soviet Government in its people. Upon leaving the Mitchells' flat, I was taken for a drive in the Squadron Leader's personal car. As soon as we drove out the gate of the apartment block, a uniformed guard stepped into a phone booth and placed a call. Moments later a small grey car fell in behind us. No matter how many twists and turns we made, the tail car never lost us.

When we stopped at a market-place, a man in a dark fedora emerged from the car behind and followed us in on foot. I began taking pictures of the colourful, innocent booths and customers. The man in the fedora made a few comments among the crowd. Soon there was an audible, hostile protest. "What are they saying?" I enquired. "They say you are a foreign spy," translated Mrs. Mitchell. We got back in the car and drove away.

Later we managed to park in the crowded area outside the American Exhibition. There was no room for the little grey car, which ran desperately up and down the street. Then the man in the fedora beckoned to a Red Army soldier passing by. After a whispered consultation, the soldier took over the pursuit.

We went into an Orthodox church at the hour of the evening service. A uniformed soldier would be too conspicuous to enter a place of religious worship. Instead, he skulked along the iron railing of the enclosure, peering through the bars. The worshippers prostrated themselves on the steps of the church as we mingled with and lost ourselves among the throng. It was an eerie and bizarre experience, yet typical of the world of phantasy in which the Soviet people live.

I had not been in Moscow many days before the heavy hand of the State was laid upon me. Oddly enough, I invited the blow myself. Soviet citizens in prominent positions are notoriously wary of foreign contacts, without official approval. Furthermore, it is very difficult to locate people, even well-known people, unless you have their addresses. So I went for help to the organization called the State Committee for Cultural Relations with Foreign Nations.

I was ushered into the office of the director of the Canadian section, Madame Ivanova, a stern-looking lady of the type that seems to fill so many positions of authority in the Soviet Union.

She did not speak to me directly, but contented herself with making quizzical and enigmatic faces at me, while her assistant, a man, did all the talking.

Far from offering me any assistance, the Committee took a very serious view of my activities in making films "for commercial purposes" without a license. I was also accused of misrepresenting myself as a tourist on entering the Soviet Union, while in reality I had come as a reporter.

This, of course, was technically true. I had applied for and got a tourist visa from the Soviet Embassy in Ottawa. Hundreds of other journalists of every nationality do the same. And, in any case, the Soviet Consul in Ottawa, giving me the visa, said to me himself, "You are going as a tourist, but you are also a reporter and can report on what you see."

Next I was directed to Sov-Export Films for a license. The director was a man who spoke no English. A young lady of the dedicated type was called in to translate. The interview got off to a bad start when I was told that Sov-Film had the sole right to take film in the Soviet Union. I pointed out that reporters anywhere in the world can take their own news film. "We are not interested in how other nations conduct their affairs," was the reply. No license was forthcoming.

It was suggested that as my film was for television I should apply to Mr. Alexander Alexandrov of Moscow Radio and TV, whom I had met on my previous visit to Moscow. An appointment was made for two o'clock in the afternoon. I presented myself duly at the Moscow Radio building and called his office on the porter's telephone. I was then informed that Mr. Alexandrov had been taken ill and gone to the country. He never was "in" to me again.

The motive behind this manoeuvring cannot be determined for sure. But I will say what I believe it was. Foreigners are welcome in the Soviet Union so long as they are useful. Hundreds of visitors from Western countries, particularly specialists in certain cultural fields, receive preferential treatment and go away entranced with the courtesy of Soviet officialdom. Such people, of course, are interested primarily in cultural matters and are themselves deeply impressed with the emphasis placed by the State on culture. They return home strong advocates of enlightened Soviet policy in their particular field.

The State, however, is not interested in facilitating or extending contact between foreigners and ordinary Soviet citizens for the purpose of a genuine exchange of ideas and information on a broad basis. Mr. Khrushchov expressed himself on this point in no uncertain terms, in his speech at Krasnoyarsk on October 9, 1959: "Can we agree to this? Of course not! Our people do not want to eat bad food poisoned with the venom of bourgeois ideas. Let us take from each other what is best, and eat yourselves your rotten goods."

Actually, I had already begun my "street meetings"—curbside debates during which Russian-speaking members of my group acted as interpreters — on the subjects of free speech, the party system of government, and the Berlin crisis. The reaction of the Russian people to these meetings was undoubtedly the crux of the whole affair. It showed that the average citizen is hungry for contact with the outside world, that he is open-minded on most questions, and is disposed to think for himself. Forty years of exposure to the most gigantic propaganda machine the world has ever known has not quenched the human spark—the spark that prompts them to doubt and question. This was the most encouraging single milestone on this journey.

The new trend was expressed most succinctly in a conversation I had with a young Russian engineer. We met by chance on a bench in Gorki Park. "I have listened to so much propaganda," he said, "that sometimes I can't stand it any more. I am fed up with attempts to teach me what to believe. They give a picture of our life which doesn't correspond to life at all. Our news is a lie, so that we do not read the papers any more. Our films are a trick—I go and then get up in a quarter of an hour and leave. I am not against Communism or any other system. My principle now is just this: no more lies!"

I did not see Madame Ivanova and the Committee for Cultural Relations with Foreign Nations again. My contacts at the government level were at an end. We set out now on our long journey in search of the "real" Russia. The first stage was to take the overnight train to Leningrad.

Tamara, our interpreter, had made all the final arrangements. She distributed our tickets and berth allocations. She obtained our passports from the hotel safe where they were always locked up during our stay—apparently so we could not leave without her knowledge.

There seemed to have been only one oversight—her own visa. We waited a short time, while she sped to the police office to get her internal passport stamped by the appropriate authority, to permit her to accompany us to Leningrad. This formula had to be repeated in every place she went. Although assigned to watch over our group throughout the Soviet Union, Tamara had to obtain a visa for each city along the way.

Even the watchers are watched.

CHAPTER

3

NIGHT TRAIN TO LENINGRAD

The Red Arrow Express; my first glimpse of the countryside;
St. Petersburg before 1917;
the Winter Palace and the Smolny;
mass at Nikolski Cathedral;
the anti-Christian campaign;
a talk with the Metropolitan Nikolai

We board the Red Arrow Express at Leningrad Station in Moscow. The train is long, blue and sleek, in the style of European trains. On the side of our carriage, in large white characters, are the letters OK. This, incidentally, refers not to the excellence of the transportation, but to the October Revolution of 1917, after which our carriage was named.

The accommodation is in separate compartments, each with two beds, a small table and lamp, and overhead luggage racks. Music is piped in on a loud-speaker. Shortly after we pull out, tea and cakes are served by a porter. There is no restaurant car and no baggage car—all our bags are piled into our compartments on top of us.

Although night has fallen, the long midsummer twilight persists. We sit with our faces pressed to the windows, striving to catch our first glimpse of the unknown countryside. Dark and mysterious, it unrolls before us—yet there is light enough for us to distinguish its characteristic features. It is flat and wild-looking, with brooding, impenetrable forests, and never a sign of human habitation for mile after mile.

Here and there, like beleaguered outposts, the villages appear, mostly of log construction, unpainted, tumbling down—a pattern that is repeated throughout the length and breadth of the Soviet Union. Whatever progress the Revolution has brought to Russia, it is evidently not in the countryside that we are to look for it. Poverty and misery have been the lot of the peasantry since the Slavic peoples first settled these plains. Within the past forty years this soil has been trampled under foot by countless armies: the czarist, the revolutionaries, the collectives, the anti-collectives, the Germans, the victorious Red Army — all burning and ravaging in their turn.

But this alone does not account for the desolation we see—for these are not Soviet-built villages that are tumbling down. They are predominantly czarist still, with their log walls and crazy windows and gables at all angles; these are not metalled roads that have been broken under the treads of tanks, they are just dust roads still; no cars stand in these back yards, no gas pumps on the highways, no stores (except the collective HQ) in the village squares. Progress has not been destroyed in these villages; it never came to them at all.

In Leningrad, we put up at the Hotel de l'Europe, a former palace. Passing these portals, we find ourselves in another world —the world before the Revolution. This is St. Petersburg (as Leningrad was formerly known); the time is as late as 1916. Nothing has changed in this lobby—the red marble columns festooned with brass drapery—the velvet curtains—even the wheezing elevator marked "up only". (Does it never come down?)

The effect is uncanny. The salons, the corridors, the very bedrooms fairly bustle with ghosts. We can imagine the army officers in glittering uniforms with eagles on their epaulettes, the elegant ladies with their bird's-nest coiffures and wasp waists, the flunkeys wearing britches and stockings. Prince Felix Yusupov, he who murdered Rasputin, may drop in for a quick game of cards. Perhaps they are holding a reception for Karsavina, the prima ballerina, who is dancing Swan Lake at the Mariinsky Theatre. Think of it! The Empress herself, Alexandra Feodorovna—granddaughter of Queen Victoria—taking tea in one of these reception rooms. . .

Was it really forty-three years ago? In the drawing-room of my suite this world of czarist Russia would be perfectly at home. The stuffed chairs and roll-end couch are in their accustomed place. The rug lies as usual across the walnut table. The Cupids continue chasing one another around the marble lamp, with its gold-fringed shade of orange silk. The marble clock with the bronze nude draped across it is still ticking on the mantle. Even the ornate Romanoff plumbing wheezes efficiently in the bathroom, and there is a coronet on the toilet bowl.

Has nothing changed in St. Petersburg since 1917? I slip out unobtrusively, without a guide, to see for myself. Again the same uncanny impression. Not one of these buildings in the parks or squares, or even along the busiest part of the Nevsky Prospekt, the main thoroughfare of the czarist capital, has been torn down or rebuilt. The city built by Peter the Great is a European city, in strong contrast to the heavy Asiatic look of the Russian hinterland. But it is the Europe of another era; the baroque churches, aristocratic avenues, and ornate elegance designed by Rastrelli, the court architect, look strangely incongruous in the Communist Russia of 1959.

From old photographs I can recognize the exact scene of the barricades of the 1905 Revolution, the shop fronts and lamp posts as they were. The very cobblestones before the Winter Palace are the same on which the *moujiks* knelt that January day, two hundred thousand of them, carrying ikons and pictures of the Czar. At their head an Orthodox priest, Father Gapon, held aloft a petition to the Czar begging for bread, a minimum wage of a rouble a day (then about fifty cents) and a people's parliament. The Czar's soldiers opened fire. Back through the streets retreated the screaming, struggling mob, carrying their thousands of wounded into the labyrinthine depths of St. Petersburg. On the cobblestones before the Winter Palace, that bloody Sunday, lay the five hundred dead.

Of such stuff are revolutions made. When the real storm broke, twelve years later in 1917, it was not led by a gentle Orthodox priest. The hard men who directed the Communist revolution from their captured headquarters in the Smolny Institute in a suburb of Petrograd were of a different sort. They did not petition the Czar, carrying ikons. The American correspondent, John Reed, a Bolshevik sympathizer, has left this vivid record of Smolny in those days:

> As night fell, the great hall filled with soldiers and workmen, a monstrous dense mass, deep humming in a blue haze of smoke. . . .
> At last Lenin got up to speak. He stood there, gripping the edge of the reading-stand, letting his little winking eyes travel over the crowd . . . apparently oblivious to the long rolling ovation, which lasted several minutes. When it finished he said simply, "We shall now proceed to construct the Socialist order."

It is only when one travels the short distance between these two focal points of power, the Winter Palace and the Smolny, that one fully understands the why of Communism. For the distance is more than a few miles by street-car from the Palace Square to the Square of the Proletariat Dictatorship; it is the swing of a great pendulum. Both were extremes—the extreme of autocratic power, based on the "divine right of kings", and the extreme of proletarian dictatorship. Neither shared in the forward-moving trend toward a broad-based society, comprising many classes, freely interchangeable but governed by a growing sense of social responsibility.

To a visitor from outside, therefore, the Communist world seems almost oppressively over-simplified—narrow, spare, stark, limited in possibility, one-sided in its exclusive emphasis on working-class consciousness. It is a world without any sense of the immense variety, the capability for both joy and sorrow, that we know.

But no society can remain fixed in a prescribed attitude, even a Communist society. Ferment starts within, eating away the core of autocratic power until only the shell is left. Already the reaction has begun to work upon the new order in Russia. We may only guess how long it will be before it reaches the surface.

The Winter Palace is a vast, rambling, baroque structure of green walls with white decoration, rather like a ginger-bread palace from a fairy tale. Today it is turned into a museum and art gallery. Inside, that haunting feeling of the closeness of the Revolution comes back.

Perhaps it is the throngs of people roaming aimlessly around the marble halls. Soldiers in shabby, ill-fitting uniforms clatter in their heavy boots over the parquet floors. Women and children in shawls and peasant dress, carrying bread wrapped in newspaper for their lunch, squat on the grand staircase under the crystal chandeliers. One has the feeling that the Imperial Family has just left hurriedly and the servants have taken over the master's hall.

The collections reflect the not altogether impeccable taste of their owners. The preference of the Romanoffs was for large, fleshy nudes of the late-Renaissance schools, and a great many second-rate landscapes. There is, however, a wonderful Rembrandt collection—none of which seems to have fallen victim to the passion for cleaning shown by most Western galleries. All the deep shadows remain; only the varnish is treated by a process that turns it clear (at least, that is how a guide explained it to me at the museum).

The Soviet taste is even more arbitrary than that of its predecessors. The emphasis is all on the literal and reproductive— battle scenes, historic figures, "social studies". The famed impressionist and post-impressionist collections have been banished to the attic, where they can be found only with difficulty. A trickle of people, mostly foreigners, mounts the narrow stairway to the poorly lit rooms that display the masterpieces of Monet, Cézanne and Gauguin.

In a window-seat, I sat beside a young Czech artist who was sketching from a Piscasso original. (Although he is a Communist, Picasso's art is still officially condemned.) He told me that things were much freer in Czechoslovakia ("out of thirteen million people we have no more than one million Communists") and modern art is freely practised there. In Russia it is still forbidden. Russian artists who want to work in these styles have to display their work secretly, he said.

I was astonished to hear that many exhibitions were held nevertheless, "in cellars and back rooms" where artists congregate. The young Czech identified several artists who were doing "outstanding work" in the modern idiom—but he thought it better I did not give their names. Some artists, he said, have even designed stage settings for "unofficial" theatre productions! True or not, I left the Hermitage strangely bemused to think that such a conversation had taken place at all.

The most beautiful buildings of Leningrad, and indeed of all Russia, are the churches. Nearly every square is a setting for a baroque structure with its amazing onion-cupolas surmounted by crosses hung with gold chains. Yet all these churches, the official guides tell you, are closed.

And so, at first, it seems. Across the entrance of the incredibly ornate Church on Blood (it was erected on the site of the assassination of Alexander II in 1881), women washing clothes in the canal near by have strung a clothes-line. Stores and gasoline stations have been cut into other churches, or they are used as museums or lumber rooms. "Religion," they say, "is dead." But is it?

If you get up early on a Sunday morning and follow the trickles of people along the street, you will find your way to the churches that are not closed. One of these is Nikolsky Cathedral. As I walked through the massive gates and approached the apse of the church, a glory of gold and green and white, I was jostled by a curious throng. Most were very old women in knee-high boots, aprons, and babushkas, pathetic remnants of Old Russia. They had been treading this path every Sunday morning, I realized, for sixty or seventy years—as though the Revolution had never been.

The spectacle on the front steps was like some scene from *Boris Godounov*. The worshippers prostrated themselves on the pavement and on each of the steps in turn, bowing their foreheads to the ground and crossing themselves many times before entering the door. The interior was ablaze with candles, rising in terraces in front of the multitude of ikons. It was packed to suffocation, no one could move, and those who were pressed closest to the ikons kissed them fervently, with eyes closed, in an ecstasy of faith.

The priest celebrated the service in a heavy gold vestment, encrusted with flashing stones. The crowd made all the responses, following the intricate intervals of the Eastern rite, without books. Many, no doubt, could not read but knew the responses by heart.

I soon felt faint, overcome by the incense, the body odour, the extraordinary intensity of the whole experience. Which was real in Russia today, I asked myself—Lenin or Christ? True, there were not many young people. Then I remembered that no member of the Communist Party may be a church-goer, and attendance at service might well deprive a younger man of a livelihood.

I squeezed my way outside again into the morning sunlight. A young man was standing at the cathedral gates. He was a student of English, so we fell into conversation. In his hand he carried a book, the covers carefully wrapped in a Russian newspaper. At my request, he showed it to me. It was an English edition, evidently smuggled into Russia, entitled *Why I Believe in God*.

Kazan Cathedral, on the Nevsky Prospekt, is a different kind of church. At least, it serves another faith. Outwardly, all appears normal—the double colonnade, the soaring dome, though I noticed this last was not surmounted by a cross. Inside, however, comes a surprise. Gone are the ikons, the crucifixes, the sad-eyed Byzantine Mother and Child. In their place are model *sputniks* and atomic plants, books by international authors from Voltaire to Huxley designed to disprove the tenets of organized religion. This building, once a Russian Orthodox Cathedral, has been turned into an anti-Christian museum.

Downstairs in the crypt is the knock-out— a life-sized representation of the Spanish Inquisition, with waxen inquisitors heating over a coal fire instruments of torture, to be applied to a victim on a bed of nails. Here we see the thumb-screws, the tongue-slicer, the collar of nails, all labelled "original specimens".

The propaganda is not all directed against religion; it has also political overtones. In the crypt is a model church that has been constructed entirely of bombs, each labelled with the names of Krupp, Vickers, Morgan, and other Western arms manufacturers. Overhead is a plaque inscribed in Russian with an excerpt from a speech by Nikita Khrushchov of December 15, 1958: "While making plans for an atomic war, the leaders of the aggressive Atlantic bloc are making pretensions of praying for peace."

There is no doubt that such propaganda has made great inroads in the minds of the younger generation. Marx, who called religion "the opium of the people", believed it would wither away before the steady advance of scientific materialism. This has not apparently taken place, and so the anti-religious propaganda has moved into high gear.

But propaganda, like everything in excess, produces its own reaction. While we were looking at the exhibits in the anti-Christian cathedral, an incident occurred. A woman in a group of Russian tourists began to protest. Her words were translated by one of the Russian-speaking members of my own group. "It

is all lies, lies! Our religion is not like that," she said. This woman was shushed by the official guide, but was afterwards engaged by us in conversation. "I cannot speak," she said,
weeping, "I shall be persecuted." A man in plain clothes then
came up and sent her away. "Look here," he said sharply,
"it is not permitted to start any propaganda in this building!"
The Soviet mind is apparently impervious to irony.

Many weeks later, I referred to this incident in a talk with His
Eminence, the Metropolitan Nikolai of the Russian Orthodox
Church. We were walking in the garden of the Patriarchate in
Moscow.

"Let them make their propaganda," exploded the kindly,
white-bearded prelate. "I make mine!"

The Orthodox Church in Russia has come through a trial
by fire since the Revolution. As soon as the Soviets came to
power, all ecclesiastical property was nationalized, and clergy
were disfranchized and deprived of the possibility of securing a
livelihood. The use of churches was permitted, but such stag-
gering charges for insurance were imposed that many congrega-
tions were unable to retain use of the buildings. So the churches
began to close.

In the dark years that followed, all teaching of religion was
forbidden. The Constitution of the Russian Soviet Federated
Socialist Republic reserved the right of propaganda to the anti-
religious forces, and the Government went all out for every
form of atheistic indoctrination. But, the Metropolitan told me,
the faith was kept alive in the homes and passed on from parents
to children. Then, after the German invasion, a new policy towards religion was inaugurated. Many churches were reopened
and prayers were offered for the defense of the country. The
Metropolitan cited many of the new cities of Soviet Asia where
new churches are going up.

After the war, the Government established an office for the
supervision of religious affairs. Thus a direct relationship between Church and State has been re-established. The nature of

the relationship is obscure. The Metropolitan asserts that the church is entirely independent, receiving no support from the state. But many of his own pronouncements are in line with official policy—for example, the church attacked the role of America, "which disturbed peaceful Hungary".

At the same time, the Soviet Government has stepped up its anti-religious crusade, making the teaching of atheism obligatory in all schools and youth organizations, thus playing both sides of the game at once. The church apparently accepts the situation, in order to gain time and fight for life.

"Meanwhile," the old Metropolitan told me, with a wry smile, as he walked among the carefully tended flower beds of his garden, "do not doubt that we shall survive. Our church is one of the oldest in Christendom. We shall go on, from ages unto ages!"

CHAPTER

4

THE SILENT SPEAK

A chance meeting;
the workers' flats; bread and vodka;
working conditions and attitudes;
how "socialist emulation" works;
Communism and freedom—can they go together?
other contacts: Komsomols, provocateurs, street meetings

It was a rainy afternoon and I sought the shelter of the colonnade outside the Antichrist Cathedral in Leningrad. My spirits, which always fluctuate with the barometer, were low. Pigeons roosting on the entablature let their droppings fall on the walk. A few lovers sat on the base of the columns, undemonstratively holding hands. The people passing by on the street sauntered as they always do, although it was raining and none wore raincoats. They looked cold, wet through, and uncommunicative. How could I hope to break through the façade of their reserve, and enter into their lives?

Then I saw a familiar face—Jack MacMillan of London, Ontario, a member of my group. He had two young men, both Russians, with him.

"These boys want to talk to you," he said and discreetly slipped away.

The elder boy bowed in a courtly way. "I am Anton," he said.

He was about twenty-eight, fair-haired, extremely neatly dressed, wearing rimless spectacles.

"Boris," said the other. He was a little younger, darker and more plainly dressed. We shook hands.

"You speak English," I said. "Are you students?"

"Not exactly," replied Anton. "We study English at home. We listen to the radio. We read English books. Your friend said you had some books we could borrow. We need English books very badly. . ."

His voice trailed away as the security policeman, on duty outside the cathedral, passed by.

"Let's take a walk," I suggested.

We started off down the Nevsky Prospekt, towards the Neva River. Anton, the elder of the two, turned out to be an engineer in a chemical plant. Boris was a worker in the same factory. Both spoke excellent English. When I explained I was a journalist, we fell at once into a discussion of newspapers.

Anton insisted there was no freedom of the press in the Soviet Union. To test him, I said I knew a Soviet journalist who assured me he could write as he pleased, without censorship. I had in fact been told this many times by members of the Soviet press corps.

"Then he told you a lie!"

"How do you know this?" I persisted.

"I know what everybody knows." There was more than a trace of bitterness in his voice. It seemed that somehow I had slipped through the façade. . . .

The rain was beating hard in our faces. "Let's go to my place," said Anton. We turned into a side street and found a taxi-cab. Boris whispered into my ear, "Don't talk English," and we got in. They gave the driver an address and we set out across the city.

The boys talked and joked in Russian. I caught the driver looking at me quizzically several times in the rear-view mirror. At last we drew up outside a movie theatre. The boys paid the driver and we went inside the vestibule. As soon as the cab had driven away, we came out again. We began walking, turning up this street and down that.

Impossible as it seems, we talked mostly about religion along the way. Both the Russians were atheists, but open-minded.

"How can you believe in God, after *sputnik?*" said Anton.

I explained that many of the leading Western scientists believe in God. This astonished and deeply impressed them. "What is the truth about religion in Russia?" I asked. "Is there any real swing over to the Church among Soviet youth?"

"It is true there is an increase in attendance on some occasions," answered Boris. "But I don't think this is significant. For example, in the country, whole villages drop their work to celebrate religious holidays. But I think this is just an excuse to drink and enjoy themselves."

The streets became narrower and more unkempt, the sidewalks disappeared, and we walked on the cobblestones. The houses on both sides were tenements four stories high, a bare bulb burning behind many of the windows, as it was growing dark. Each window, they told me, represented one family.

We turned into an unlighted hallway and climed three flights of stone stairs in a dark stairwell. On the top floor we reached the door of Anton's flat. It was shared by three families, he explained—his parents, his own family and one other. He cursed when he found he had forgotten his key.

He rang the bell and asked me to step out of sight when the door opened. A young girl answered. After a few words in Russian, the girl disappeared and they signalled me to enter the flat. I found myself in a narrow hall, with three doors opening off it. The room at the end was Anton's. It was tiny but very neat. There was a folding bed, a rug on the wall, a small round table and two chairs, a dressing-table, a radio-phonograph, and a stove burner in a closet.

Anton lived here with his wife, who was away with her parents in the country, expecting a child. The room was "safe", I was told, as one wall adjoined Anton's parents and the others were outside walls, so no one could hear us.

I asked how much the rent was for his room, unfurnished.

"Sixty roubles ($6) a month, but then, as you see, it is very small."

And how much did he earn?

"As an engineer I make 1,200 roubles a month. From that subtract 12 per cent income tax deducted at source. I clear only 1,000 roubles ($100)."

For this what could he buy?

"If a person lives moderately he has to spend 400 roubles a month for food alone for each person in the family. Clothes are expensive—1,600 roubles for a suit of clothes, 400 roubles for a pair of shoes."

I remarked that this was already several times more than he earned in a month. So what did he do?

"The solution is for two in every family to work."

The boys now opened the cupboard and brought out black bread and cucumbers and vodka. They made a little spread on the table and we sat down to eat. Vodka is extremely strong to our taste, but the Russian habit is to drink down a glass at one throw. Every time I failed, they insisted on filling it up and urging me to try again!

What would happen, I wanted to know, if the police did discover our meeting?

"Now it wouldn't hurt us," Anton replied. "But we would be ear-marked and it would lead to a lack of trust. When the chance came to escape to the West, perhaps on some delegation, we would not be chosen."

"Are Soviet people, then, afraid to associate with Westerners?"

"Yes, because they are afraid the line might change."

"Do most people in Russia realize the difference between their standard of living and ours?"

"Some do. But not most. They have no information. Two years ago the *New York Times* used to be available in the public library—it is not now. I went to read it every day. I put down prices. I calculated what it meant for every item. If your worker gets $300 a month, he can buy 100 shirts with that. A Russian worker would have to pay 25,000 roubles for 100 shirts —at 1,000 roubles a month pay, it would take him over two years. But when I gave my figures to my fellow workers, nobody would believe me that the gap was so great."

"We hear much about the work of the Soviet people in exceeding their quotas," I said. "What is the truth about this?"

"That is all trash. Socialist emulation, they call it. I know that workers only work for money. I don't know why they pretend."

"How does this principle of socialist emulation work?"

"Well, most workers get extra pay for hard work. But if a worker begins to earn 1,500 roubles a month, his hourly rate of pay is cut to bring his pay down to 1,200 roubles, so he will have to work harder next month. Now we know better than to earn too much. After reaching 1,200 roubles we just stop working and start idling and drinking, so the rates will not be cut. That's how socialist emulation works!"

"Nevertheless, we hear there has been an enormous increase in productivity in the Soviet Union. How do you account for that?"

"The increase is due to capital investment by Government in industry, such as new chemical plants, and is not due to greater output on the part of the workers."

"Mr. Khrushchov says Russia will overtake the USA by 1972 —do you believe this?"

"So far I don't notice any increase in our standard of living. Anyhow, Mr. Khrushchov admits that productivity in our country is three times less than in the USA."

"Why do you think he admits this?"

"He begins to tell the truth. Maybe that is why we begin to like Mr. Khrushchov."

"Why do you think the Government is afraid to let you get information? Because, if the truth were known, Communism would be overthrown?"

"No!" exclaimed Boris.

"So you are a good Communist in spite of all you have told me, Boris?"

"I love my country," said Boris slowly, "but I do not shut my eyes to the mistakes in our system which should be removed."

"You think it is just a question of mistakes and not principles?"

"Yes, I think the principles of Communism are quite right."

"Then why do you think capitalism has produced the better standard of living?"

"I think it is because our system is a new one and there are bound to be some difficulties at first."

"Do you believe you can have Communism and freedom at the same time?"

"Yes. It must be so."

"You are an idealist, Boris. What do other Russian workers think about this?"

"I have had many talks with workers in our country," replied Anton, "because my work has taken me all over the Soviet Union—and I know this: nobody cares a hang about socialist emulation any more—only about how to keep body and soul together."

So we talked, far into the night. It was a late hour when I left. Boris and Anton took me back to my hotel by the same circuitous method; we walked for a half dozen blocks, took a cab nearer the city centre, then walked some more till we reached a park near the hotel.

On the way, Anton had pressed me for any literature I had in English, even a dictionary. I picked up an Oxford dictionary, a couple of paper-backed novels, and a Canadian Government pamphlet, *Canada from Sea to Sea*.

I returned to the park and found them strolling about. When they caught sight of me they sauntered off up the street, I following. After a block or so, they turned into an apartment doorway. I found them inside in an unlighted hall. In the dark we said our good-byes. I gave Anton the books and Boris my lighter.

Not all meetings with the Russian people were so easy. *Agents provocateurs* now began to dog my steps. The first was a young man by the name of Theodore. He joined me at my table in the hotel dining-room one day, saying he was a student and wanted to talk.

He certainly talked—loudly criticizing the Government for corruption, bribery, and fraud, but giving few details. Then he began questioning me about what I knew, where I had been, whom I had met. I was non-committal. He became provocative. "You cannot be a very good journalist," he said, "if you know so little!"

Apparently my movements were not entirely known, since it was deemed advisable to set informers of this type on me. I drew what comfort I could from this. But on reflection I decided that I must excercise the utmost caution in my encounters with Soviet people.

Another type I learned to beware of was the Komsomol Youth. This organization, comprising students dedicated to Communism, was evidently commissioned to keep watch over the foreigners. They congregated around the Intourist hotels in every city, frequently coming up and engaging in conversation, in an aggressive manner.

"Why are the Western Powers preparing for war?"

"Why do you surround us with bases?"

"Why don't you disarm?"

It is possible that some tourists might be impressed, on meeting such persons, that they are making contact with real Soviet opinion. I would be inclined to discount all such contacts. At no time did I encounter hostile or critical opinion among real Soviet people. Indeed, the agents of the official party line were strictly avoided, and even sometimes exposed, by plain folk.

An interesting example of this kind of by-play took place one evening in Pushkin Square. A group of American students visiting Russia, the Russian Club of Yale, were gathering each evening at the base of Pushkin's monument to sing American spirituals and other songs. This brought out large crowds and was usually followed by lively discussions. I soon found myself the centre of an interested group who asked me shyly about my ball-point pen, my job, and my home, in halting English.

Suddenly a young, loud-voiced student took over. He spoke good English and began asking a different line of question.

"Is it possible to buy *New Times* [the Soviet magazine published in English] in Canada?"

I said it was possible but you would not find it on the street corner. This he interpreted to mean that Soviet literature was banned in Canada.

"Do you read our great Soviet authors?"

I said the last book I had read was *Dr. Zhivago*, by Boris Pasternak.

"That is a bad book," asserted my youthful interlocutor.

I asked him how he knew this, seeing the book was banned in Russia.

He replied, "I have read in *Pravda* that it is a libel on the Soviet way of life. So I know that it is a bad book."

I said we believed that people should be able to read what they liked and make up their own minds about it. This brought a slight applause from the crowd, which showed that many did understand English and supported me against my young antagonist.

On the defensive now, he asked me what I admired most in the Soviet Union. I answered, "The Soviet people."

"How about our *sputniks*?"

I replied that they were indeed a great achievement, but mentioned that the United States too was experimenting in this field.

"Yes—with baby *sputniks*!" he jeered.

I inquired why the Soviet Union had spent so much on the development of *sputniks* and so little on making more cars available for the people.

This was due, he said, to the great devastation caused by the war, which destroyed the factories and the materials.

"Yes," I said, "but we would put the autos first and the *sputniks* last!"

Again a round of applause, which left no doubt this time where the sympathies of the people were.

There were several such public meetings and personal contacts during my stay in Leningrad. Frequently, when the crowd dispersed, I would be followed by a small group of Russians who wanted to talk privately. Usually they had the same criticisms to make about restrictions on freedoms.

They complained that American broadcasts in the Russian language were jammed, although apparently American broadcasts in English were getting through all right. This was interpreted as a sign that Mr. Khrushchov bows to the will of the new intelligentsia, who have learned English and who would regard jamming of English broadcasts as a personal affront.

They were hungry for books, magazines, and news from the West, and they deeply resented the regulations that prevented them from obtaining such literature. They wanted passionately to travel outside their country, but could not do so because exit visas are never granted for personal reasons, only for the purposes of the State. Soviet citizens may not, in fact, travel *inside* the Soviet Union without the formality of a visa obtained from the police.

So far, these criticisms seemed directed mainly against the bureaucracy of the régime. I never encountered any criticism of Communism. But perhaps this would be expecting too much. Most of this criticism is naïve—it does not challenge the basic premise of state dictatorship, yet expects to enjoy the privileges of a free society.

The most important single impression formed by these contacts was the friendliness and open-mindedness towards the West and Western ideas. Forty years of propaganda have not suceeded in turning the Soviet people against the West. In spite of all they hear and read every day, there is no sign that they regard us as aggressive, hostile or wicked. They admire our standard of living, our basic freedoms; above all they want to share with us in the great adventure of making a better life.

Many Soviet people believe sincerely that this day will come, when our two systems can go hand in hand together down the road of human progress. They see in the present relaxation of some of the rigours of the Stalinist régime an evolution toward greater tolerance and freedom in the Soviet Union. It is just a question of time, they say.

Others are not so convinced. Among these were two young students encountered by another member of our group, Fred Peel of Stratford, Ontario. Mr. Peel is the owner of a successful shoe factory. He urged his young Russian friends to make their way to Canada, where he promised to sponsor them in new jobs. Their reaction was unexpected. Both wept, and confessed that such a solution to their hopes was impossible.

"Only bad Russians are allowed out of Russia," said one. "For us there is no hope!"

5

A FORBIDDEN JOURNEY

The disappearance of Uno Kingisepp; his background;
Estonia: a captive people,
exploring the streets of Tallin; are we prisoners?
present-day conditions in Estonia;
Kingisepp's return and our release; new questions are raised

We were finishing breakfast one morning in the dining-room of the Hotel de l'Europe. Tamara, our official interpreter, came over to me and asked: "Where is Mr. Kingisepp?" His chair was still empty. "Probably overslept," I replied. "I'll wake him."

But there was no answer to my knock at his room door. I took the key from the porter's desk and let myself in. The room was empty, the bed not slept in. On the table was a note:

"I have gone away. I'm sorry if I have caused any trouble. I will try to join the group later.

Uno Kingisepp."

Quietly, I locked the door again and returned to the dining-room. "Mr. Kingisepp is not well today," I said. "We'll have to go on our tour without him." Tamara seemed unconcerned.

Uno Kingisepp was an Estonian by birth. His father and his forefathers before him were landowners in free Estonia. In the summer of 1944, Uno was just out of school, at seventeen. As a graduation gift, the Germans, who then occupied the country, sent him his call-up papers.

Uno left home and hid in the woods. There he was joined by forty of his schoolmates who did not want to serve in a foreign army. They found an abandoned boat on the beach and equipped it with a motor from an army truck stolen from under the noses of the Germans. One moonless night, they pushed off across the Baltic for neutral Sweden. The boat was old and it sprang so many leaks that the escape party had to bail for their lives. Gradually, the water rose faster than they could bail, and after two hours they had to turn back.

A further agonizing week in hiding went by, while they patched and mended the boat; then came the second attempt. This time they succeeded in reaching a Swedish island, 180 miles away. Not content with this feat, however, young Uno returned with his boat a total of four times across the Baltic, to rescue his mother and father and hundreds of his countrymen.

Altogether, more than thirty thousand Estonians made their way that moonless September to the safety of Sweden. Of these, about seventeen thousand came to Canada. Among them was Uno Kingisepp. He settled down and took out citizenship papers. But he could not forget his homeland, now engulfed by the advancing Soviet tide. He wanted to go back—if only for a glimpse. He sold his house in Toronto and joined my tour.

The story of the Estonians is the story of all the captive peoples in the Soviet Union. It is perhaps insufficiently realized that the Russians are themselves in a minority in their own country. While the Russian Soviet Federated Republic dominates all other groups, it is itself outnumbered by the captive peoples—the Ukrainians, Uzbeks, Armenians, Tajiks, Moldavians, Lithuanians, Latvians, Estonians, and others—who willingly or otherwise form part of the USSR. In each and every case, these were peoples who cherished their independence and fought against the Russians to retain it. The imbalance represents a grave weakness of the Soviet system, and carries within it the seed of of dissolution.

It could hardly be maintained, unless all the world's history books are to be burned or travestied, that the peoples of the Baltic states joined the Soviet Union gladly. For centuries subject to foreign yoke, they kept the flame of liberty alive in their hearts and brought it out into the open in 1918. The independent republics of Lithuania, Latvia and Estonia, established by the Treaty of Versailles, were beacons in the dark history of oppression and slavery.

All the world applauded the heroism of these people, their industry and prosperity. A British stateman, the late Lord Wedgewood, called Estonia "the best-governed small nation in Europe". But all to no avail. In the holocaust of 1939, their short-lived independence was extinguished. After the division of spoils agreed upon by Hitler and Stalin, the Baltic States fell under Soviet occupation.

The first Soviet occupation of Estonia in 1940 lasted fourteen months. Soviet authorities acted quickly to destroy all political, economic and cultural life of the country. The President of the Republic and many other leaders were deported to Siberia. Nearly two thousand Estonians were murdered and over 100,000 men, women and children dispersed to other parts of the Soviet Union. The Estonian nation was systematically destroyed.

This was followd by three years of German occupation as the Wehrmacht rolled across Europe. But the Germans proved as hard masters as the Soviets, plundering and looting the country for themselves. And with the second Soviet occupation in 1944, the liquidation of the last vestiges of Estonia's economic and cultural life took place. Estonian agriculture was collectivized, industry reorganized to serve the needs of the Soviet Union, the standard of living, once one of the highest in Europe, brought down to the average Soviet level.

I began making enquiries among the other members of the group about Uno Kingisepp's disappearance. Soon I had several important facts. At 11:30 the preceding night two of the Russian-speaking members of our group had accompanied him to the railroad station and bought him a ticket to Tallinn, the capital of Soviet-ruled Estonia. His own command of Russian was evidently not good enough to risk this alone.

"But, good heavens!" I exclaimed, "don't you know that Tallinn is a forbidden area?" Actually, 40 per cent of the Soviet Union is out of bounds to foreigners. Estonia is also a separate Soviet Republic, with its own border check-points. It seemed unlikely that he would get through without a visa.

Surprisingly enough, he did. Later, Uno told his own story. It was a Sunday night, he said, and the train was filled with holiday-makers, mostly Estonians, returning from a week-end in Leningrad. The journey took seven hours. On the way, Uno talked little and soon fell asleep, sitting up in his corner of the carriage. They passed through the border point at dawn. Perhaps the guards were asleep, too, because they waved the train on without an individual passport check.

In Tallinn, Uno said, he could pass unnoticed. He wandered freely through the city all day, during which time apparently no police followed him. The people in the streets seemed poorly dressed and wore an indifferent air he did not remember. He removed his own jacket and tie and scuffed his shoes, so as not to attract attention.

Everywhere he noticed sad changes from the country he remembered. In the countryside, farm buildings were often deserted, tumbling down, the roofs fallen in. In the capital, the pavement seemed all torn up—"They said they were laying new sewers, but I don't know," Uno commented.

Everywhere many Russians, both soldiers and civilians, seemed to be in evidence—something unheard of before the occupation. Even the street signs were in Russian now as well as Estonian.

The atmosphere had changed too. Uno sought out his former

haunts. He went down to the beach, and stopped at the well-known Piriea restaurant for a glass of beer. This was the only place where an attempt was made to keep up appearances. The patrons seemed to be mostly Russian party officials. At the equally famous Viru's cafe, where the "best people" used to congregate for a social evening, everything was now run down and seedy—even the waiters displayed a two-day growth of beard.

Tallin, Uno found, has suffered the fate of every European capital that has fallen to the Communist tide. The bright lights have been extinguished, the coloured parasols and awnings over the sidewalk cafés have been folded up and put away, the displays of goods in the stores have disappeared; the hubbub of traffic, the eager pushfulness of passers-by, the hum of a great city, have all stopped like a clock run down.

Two days passed and still Uno did not appear. In Leningrad, of course, I had no idea what had happened to him. It seemed strange that the Soviet authorities had displayed no interest whatsoever in his absence. Tamara, the interpreter, had discreetly refrained from making any more enquiries. The police had never been around to ask the usual routine questions about when and where he was last seen.

All this led me to believe that the Russians had their information and were already on his track. Perhaps by this time they had captured him! Perhaps he was being interrogated by the secret police!

Then another strange thing happened. Our tour ground to a stop. On Monday, the day after Uno's disappearance, we were scheduled to leave by plane for Kiev. We packed and checked out of our rooms. We climbed aboard the bus drawn up outside the hotel, but we did not leave. They said the plane was late.

Several hours passed. We were told not to get out of the bus "in case the plane arrives". An Intourist guide stood guard outside at all times. By nightfall I insisted on re-engaging the rooms, if possible, for the night. None of the rooms had been taken, even though the hotel was crowded.

Next day, the comedy was repeated. We were told to wait in the bus. Tamara was at the telephone, hour by hour, "talking with the airport", now hopeful, now dejected about the prospects of getting away. Finally, I put the question that was in all minds: were we prisoners? There was no reply. I noticed that Tamara had taken off her maple-leaf pin!

It was then I decided to call the Canadian Embassy in Moscow. Fortunately I had the number in my notbook, because it is not listed in the telephone directory and the information service never gives you a number, if you do not know it—part of the secrecy of everyday life in the Soviet Union.

I spoke with the First Secretary and acquainted him with the facts. I realized that the line was certainly tapped, but there was no doubt that the Soviet authorities already knew more than I did about Kingisepp's disappearance. The Embassy promised to take the matter up with the Soviet Foreign Office.

Meanwhile, unknown to us, Uno had given himself up. Even more surprisingly, the police did not arrest him. They examined his passport, repeatedly asked who sent him, and finally passed him to the Security Office, which issues visas. Here, Uno found himself at the end of a long queue waiting for visas to leave the country. Although exit visas from the Soviet Union are exceedingly rare, he encountered an elderly couple by chance who had just received their visas to come to Canada.

When his turn came, the woman in charge showed great surprise at his Canadian passport. She told him he should not have come to Estonia without a visa, as it is a forbidden zone. In the end, however, she relented and let him fill in an application form so he could stay overnight. And she booked him a room at the Palace Hotel.

At the hotel, another woman behind the reception desk clucked over his passport again. "Aren't you ashamed of yourself?" she enquired. "Here you are, an Estonian by birth, with a Canadian passport!"

Next day, he fell in with a young man who asked if he could show him the town. This seemed quite by chance, said Uno, but later he wondered if this man had been sent by the police to watch him. Together they visited several of the sights, including a dance-hall. The young man excused himself several times in order, he said, "to call his wife".

Uno still had his movie camera with him and he began taking pictures. People in the street noticed the camera at once and asked where he got it. Uno avoided answering their questions directly. He seemed to shy away from revealing his identity, as though he might get another wigging for not being a good Soviet citizen. He also says he had many friends and acquaintances in Tallin, but he did not look them up for fear of compromising them.

Somehow, Uno's escapade had turned out differently from what might have been expected. At first he was greatly excited to be home again; but soon this was followed by a feeling of disappointment. "This was a different Estonia," he says. "Perhaps we [Estonian Canadians] have changed without noticing it ourselves. Now we speak a different language."

On the afternoon of the second day, the police picked him up and delivered him to the airport. He was put aboard a plane for Kiev—the next stop on our official itinerary. His adventure was at an end.

Magically, about the same time, the sky suddenly cleared in Leningrad. We were rushed to the airport on half an hour's notice to catch a plane we had awaited for two days. It was a special chartered plane, with no other passengers, no stewardess, no regular equipment such as seat belts, luggage racks, or magazines.

When we arrived at Kiev, there was Uno Kingisepp. Was there a connection between his disappearance and our two-day delay? Had Intourist been notified to release us after he was found? Or was it all a comedy of errors? These are questions that will never be satisfactorily answered.

This incident, however, served to deepen the mystery into which my journey seemed to be leading me. I realized, for the first time, how little I knew about the motives within the Soviet world or the extent to which any of my companions were implicated in them.

CHAPTER

6

ACROSS THE UKRAINE

*Arrival in Kiev; Theodore Humeniuk's story;
first night in a "hard" coach;
the Ukraine, a submerged nation;
mysterious encounters in Kharkov;
a collective farm; Odessa and a night at the ballet*

The bus that was to take us from Kiev Airport into the Ukrainian capital was garlanded with flowers—so many, in fact, that there was no room to sit down. The seats were piled high with roses, gladioli and delphiniums. At first I thought this gesture of Ukrainian hospitality was intended for us. Then I learned that the bus had come out to the airport with a departing group of tourists from Communist Czechoslovakia. They left behind what they could not carry.

Quite different treatment was in store for us. As the leader of the group, I was summoned to the front of the bus by the local Intourist guide. In each place we stopped, Tamara remained in charge of the group, but a local guide took over the planning of our itinerary.

This person was a young woman of formidable proportions, severe expression, and not a trace of make-up. She informed me that there was to be no repetition of the "indiscipline" of which my group had been guilty. In future we were to stay together as a group.

Somehow, I wanted more than anything to burst out laughing. The idea that a group of Canadians, all adult, many prominent in their professions, and all paying $30 a day to Intourist for a good time, were to be hectored in this way by a young Russian girl in a polka-dot dress appeared ludicrous.

Instead, however, I merely pointed out that we were all individuals and expected to be treated as such. Furthermore, I said, there was to be no question of punishment for us, individually or as a group.

"You will do as you are told," was her reply.

Now I was not laughing. I realized that I was up against the official Soviet mind. Somehow, I felt as if all the frustration and struggle of interminable international conferences, from Panmunjom to Berlin, were represented right there in that bus. No doubt this seems overdrawn now. But that's how it seemed then.

"In that case," I replied, "my group will leave Russia."

We drove the rest of the way in silence.

One of the members of my group, Mr. Theodore Humeniuk, was looking forward with particular eagerness to this visit to Kiev. In the late years of the last century, he was born at Potochysche, a little village in the Western Ukraine, near Lvov. Before the First World War, he emigrated to Canada, where he became a successful lawyer. A brother remained behind in Potochysche, and more than anything in the world Theodore Humeniuk wanted to meet him again.

Ever since we had arrived in Russia, a barrage of letters, telegrams, and requests for a phone connection had been despatched to Potochysche—all without result. Although Mr. Humeniuk had heard frequently from his brother when in Canada, he could not seem to raise a reply in Russia.

So the first day of our visit to Kiev, we called on the Intourist chief to try to arrange a visit for Mr. Humeniuk to Potochysche. The chief was a young and agreeable man who even smiled occasionally—a rare characteristic in Soviet officialdom. He was quick to point out, however, that we were already two days behind schedule and would therefore have to leave Kiev that same evening.

"So you see there is not time to go to Potochysche," he smiled amiably.

I pointed out that our late arrival in Kiev was the fault of the Intourist organization, not of ourselves, and that Mr. Humeniuk had spent a great deal of money and travelled more than seven thousand miles to see his brother. I proposed that he should be given leave to spend two days visiting his brother and rejoin our group in Odessa.

The chief consented to this arrangement and instructed Mr. Humeniuk to wait in his hotel room until special transport had been arranged to take him to Potochysche. Back at the hotel, he tried again to reach his brother by phone. Still no result. Then, at five o'clock in the afternoon, the local guide knocked at his door. He was told to rejoin our group at once, as we were leaving for the railway station. It was too late now for appeal. The Intourist office was closed.

Bitterly, I asked the guide to make arrangements for Mr. Humeniuk to return to Moscow so he could leave Russia. I was told that no transportation was available. He must remain with the group.

The perfidy of this transaction, the arbitrary behaviour of the officials, the elusiveness of the unseen brother, all contributed to depress our spirits. It seemed as if we were like lost children, wandering in a mysterious forest, not knowing whom to trust, what to believe, or how to find our way out. We were indeed "doing what we were told," I reflected wryly!

Later, back in Moscow, when our official tour was over, Mr. Humeniuk tried once more to visit Potochysche. He bought a special three-day excursion to Kiev for himself. He asked Intourist to advise his brother of his arrival and arrange for them to meet in Kiev. This they appeared willing to do.

Mr. Humeniuk's second visit, however, was as fruitless as his first. Intourist appeared to be doing everything possible to bring the two brothers together, but in fact seemed to be only succeeding in keeping them apart. He was told that his brother came to Kiev, awaited his arrival at the wrong terminal, and went home again. No explanation was ever given why he could not visit his own home village.

Thus Theodore Humeniuk came twice to Kiev, within a hundred miles of his brother whom he had not seen since childhood, and then never saw him. Why? Like so much else in the Soviet world—why, why, why?

As a result of this *contretemps,* I was deprived of more than a fleeting glimpse of the Ukrainian capital. The broad avenues, very handsomely rebuilt since the war, the many trees and public gardens, invited a longer stay. But no deviation was permitted from the schedule.

It was raining when Tamara distributed our berth allocations on the station platform. The berths were scattered all over fifteen coaches. Each compartment was shared by four—Russians and Canadians, men and women, all mixed up together.

Some of the compartments were "soft" and some were "hard". That is to say, some had cushion seats which could be converted into beds; others had only wooden flat benches, on which one slept with only the comfort of a single blanket. About half our group drew the wooden benches. No attempt had been made to provide the ladies with the better accomodation.

It took most of the evening to sort this tangle out—with the help of obliging Russian passengers, much sign language and laughter. In the end everyone was happy. Cecil Elliott, owner of an automobile business in Woodstock, Ontario, who is on the hearty side of fifty, recalls his personal experience this way:

"There I was," he says, "with a top bunk and not even a ladder on the train. But I didn't have a bit of trouble. They put three of those big Russian girls in with me, who just heaved me up at night and lifted me down like a feather. Never spent a better night!"

It was reassuring, at least, to find that we were not as unlucky as some others. Some carriages were converted into barrack-room dormitories, in which passengers of both sexes, in various degrees of attire, were ranged on wooden benches, three deep, one above another. The atmosphere in these carriages reached the highest degree of body odour I ever recollect, and they had to be traversed with considerable care to avoid the large number of bare, sweaty feet that projected at eye-level into the passage-way.

Most of us sought the refuge of the dining-car, where the seats were at least upholstered (not everyone was lucky enough to secure one). Here we whiled away the night, talking, singing, and drinking endless glasses of tea. The chef soon ran out of supplies, but luckily he had some live hens in the galley that were induced by the noise and brightness to lay some eggs, which made an excellent snack.

By day the Ukrainian countryside rolled by the train window in endless vistas of rolling fields, golden with wheat, crowned here and there with the remnants of the ancient oak forests that were cut down long ago by the Russian invaders. The land breathes a melancholy beauty, the legacy of a tragic history.

The Ukrainians are a submerged people, one of the many that form the Soviet Union. They are the most numerous people (forty million) in Europe without a sovereign government of their own. But they are not without national aspirations and, in fact, maintain the biggest underground army of liberation of any of the submerged nations in the Soviet Union.

Not since the collapse of the great State of Kiev has the Ukraine been independent. That was seven hundred years ago. Yet this ancient civilization, flourishing in what was then the outer darkness of barbarism, gave vivid proof of the energy and originality of its culture.

The state was founded by the Great Vladimir, the Saint, (980-1015), who spread the faith as a civilizing force. Under this impetus hundreds of churches arose, with golden, glittering cupolas, many of which are still to be seen today in the city of

Kiev. Libraries compiled the learning of the ancient world, of monkish Europe and of the ascetic East. Travellers of the eleventh century admired the wealth of paintings, mosaics, gardens, and palaces.

It was also a democratic civilization, with parliamentary institutions derived from the city-states of ancient Greece, and a prince who was a warrior general, subject to the will of the people.

Suddenly, in the thirteenth century, this Golden Age was brought to a close by the invasion of the Mongols. The people of the Ukraine were never independent again. But the democratic spirit lived on among the warrior bands of Cossacks, who elected their own *hetmen,* or leaders, and never submitted to any conqueror. Time after time they rose against their masters —the Mongols, the Russians, the Poles. The last great rebellion occurred in 1709, when the Cossacks under Mazeppa joined forces with Charles XII of Sweden against Russia's Peter the Great. Peter won, at Poltava, and subdued the Ukraine with unexampled savagery.

But hope did not die. During the Communist Revolution of 1917, a strong nationalist movement swept the country, culminating in the election of a Rada (independent government) at Kiev, under the presidency of the well-known scholar and nationalist leader, Michael Hrushevsky.

On December the 17th, the Soviet Government sent an ultimatum to the Rada. Bolshevik agents organized an internal revolt and Kiev was captured by the Red Army amid an orgy of murder and pillage. The subsequent deportation and extermination of Ukrainian leaders ended all practical hope of independence.

But with each new generation hope is reborn. During the Second World War, hundred of thousands of young Ukrainians joined the UPA (Ukrainian Insurgent Army) fighting against both Nazis and Soviets. In June, 1944, a Supreme Ukrainian Council for Liberation was formed, just before the reoccupation of the Western Ukraine by Soviet troops. Its principles include "Ukrainian independence, free enterprise for the peasant on his land, free enterprise for the worker". These goals, says Clarence A. Manning in *Twentieth Century Ukraine*, are still held by all Ukrainians worthy of the name.

The extraordinary fact is that, despite the overwhelming odds, the UPA is still in action. Large detachments, armed with automatic weapons, under strict military discipline, hide out in the deep forests, conducting periodic raids, extending even into neighbouring satellite countries. Again and again the Soviet press appeals to the people not to assist them, but it is apparent that without the help of the villages they could not exist at all.

I had studied the photographs, smuggled out from their hideouts, of these freedom fighters—clean-cut, handsome, intelligent-looking boys—many of whom are listed from time to time as "killed in action". What is it they die for? They can have little hope at present of winning independence for their country. The only objective can be to maintain themselves in existence against the hypothetical day when another great conflict will shift the power balance of the world. But their very existence is extraordinary proof of the discontent that lurks at the core of the Soviet world.

Such were the thoughts uppermost in my mind as I watched the golden panorama of the Ukraine, its winding rivers and its little white villages, unroll before me.

Kharkov, another great Ukrainian city, came later in our journey, but perhaps I should deal with it here before leaving the Ukraine. This splendid city was almost totally destroyed during the twenty-two months of German occupation. Today it has risen from the ruins anew—a city of broad, handsome boulevards and the largest square in Europe, Derjinsky Square. But behind the imposing façade, life goes on here, as elsewhere in the Soviet Union, in a congeries of cramped and jostled tenements.

The Intourist hotel in which we lodged was a typical example. It was a decrepit building, with rooms opening on a filthy back yard full of broken brick, ashes, and dirt. Only three of our rooms had a bath; some had no basins. Our guide told us there just was not enough room for all the foreigners in town.

In the course of the day, I happened upon the Kharkov Hotel in Derjinsky Square, a fine new building in a good location. I enquired at the desk and was told there were nine hundred rooms, each with private bath. Price for each room was fifty roubles (five dollars) for two. The clerk said the hotel was one-third empty. The guest list included Russian, Chinese, Czechoslovak, and other Communist nationalities—but no North American guests.

From this and many other examples, I was forced to the conclusion that Western tourists are not really wanted in the Soviet Union. Contrary to popular belief in the West, Soviet officials are not out to please Westerners. It is the Communists they seek to impress. When I remarked on this to an Intourist official, I was told, "We don't care what impression you have. You are not in the Plan."

One of the principal objects of my visit was to see the farm-machinery plant for which Kharkov is famous. To my surprise, the local guide professed a complete ignorance about this factory. I continued to press the point and finally the guide conceded that there had once been such a plant in Kharkov but, he said, it had been destroyed by the Germans and never rebuilt.

The same evening, I met a group of American farmers, just arrived in Kharkov. "What are you going to see?" I enquired. They told me they were being taken to the farm-machinery plant the next morning. This kind of mystification was typical of our entire experience in the Soviet Union. But I was to hear more of this farm-machinery plant before I left Kharkov.

Meanwhile, we did get to see the electrical-appliances factory, said to employ eleven thousand people. On arrival, we were told to leave our cameras outside. I could see why as soon as we entered the plant. The floor was littered with broken equipment, disused parts, and rubbish. Every single piece of equipment, from the giant shapers down to the smallest riveters, bore an American, British or German label. Here no attempt had been made to conceal the foreign name-plates. Usually the Soviet manufacturers are very clever about this. Soviet cars are invariably copies of American models, mostly of ancient vintage, down to the last door-handle. I have seen the label **GMC** changed to read 3MC. Ford is often changed to resemble a Russian word.

But in the electrical-appliance factory at Kharkov, no such device had been employed. In fact, the foreign brass plates shone as if polished. This leads to an unresolved puzzle: far from stressing their best products, do they often show Westerners their worst? It would be as dangerous to assume that Soviet industry is as backward as this factory, as it would be to assume that Soviet listening devices are as primitive as the microphones they sell in stores.

One day, during my stay in Kharkov, I met a Russian engineer who had emigrated to Russia from Canada. I was at the soft-drink stand and he spoke to me in English. When it turned out that we were both born in Montreal, we shook hands and began to talk. Of Russian parentage, he had come to Russia in the early days of the Revolution "to help build the fatherland". He hadn't been here six weeks, he said, before he realized his mistake. But then it was too late.

Nevertheless he had made something of himself. He had a little money and he studied to become an engineer. Now he held down a good job in a factory, earning twelve hundred roubles a month. But he longed to be back in Montreal. It was a bit strange to stand under the awning of the *marojnye* (ice cream) stand in Kharhov and hear this grizzled old man recollect the charms of St. Denis Street, the Park Slide, and the hansom cabs on Mount Royal.

He told a harrowing tale of the German occupation, during the Second World War. The Germans had simply left the population to starve. In his house, six German soldiers were quartered. They ate chicken and bread with butter, but would not give even a scrap to his grandchild, who went without food for a whole week. "If the Germans had not behaved so, they might not have lost the war," he commented cryptically.

I heard this said (or rather muttered) by several people in the Ukraine. Did it mean that Ukrainians might have joined the Germans themselves in overthrowing the Communists? Some did, of course, and this led to brutal retaliation after the war. A residue of this bitterness certainly remains. Despite Soviet assertions of Ukrainian autonomy, it is very noticeable that the Ukrainian language is discriminated against in all official quarters. Ukrainian members of my group were refused permission to send telegrams written in Ukrainian. Out of twenty-three churches in Kiev now open, only one celebrates the services in the Ukrainian language.

By night, there were stranger contacts. Among the odd assortment of people who always hung around the hotel doors was a young German. He was engaged in conversation by Victor Thiessen, of Winnipeg, a member of our group of German origin. This chap, ostensibly an East German, worked in Kharkov in the farm-machinery plant.

We asked him why we had not been allowed to see it. "Perhaps you would see too much," he replied. And he went on to assert that the plant itself was only a blind for an aircraft factory located directly beneath it.

"You want to see the town?"

We climbed into a taxi and he gave some addresses. Driving through the darkened streets, he pointed out a succession of curious sights. Later, when the cab was dismissed, he told us more about them.

There were the red-brick walls of the farm-machinery plant, which did seem to have a surprising lot of armed guards about the gate. There was a barracks where, he said, several hundred civilians lived who worked in the underground aircraft plants. They always left and returned in a bus with the blinds drawn and guarded by soldiers. There was a huge area of the town, clearly sealed off by barbed wire that we were told was electrified. This, he asserted, was an "atom town", where seven or eight thousand prisoners were employed in nuclear work.

Kharkov, of course, is known to be an important industrial centre and it would be surprising indeed if there were not a number of armament plants. But somehow I did not expect to see them in quite this way. I have no means of knowing, of course, if our young friend was telling the truth, or why he conducted us on this bizarre tour. But it confirmed my suspicion that much more lies hidden in the Soviet world than we can ever fathom.

Arriving in Odessa District, in the southern Ukraine, we switched to a bus, in order to visit a collective farm. The road was one of those charming Russian roads that wander apparently aimlessly across the countryside. Although a main highway, judging by the heavy load of telephone wires alongside, it was unsurfaced throughout a full day's journey.

These roads do not follow any philosophy of travel known to us. Sometimes the road will broaden to three times its normal size, often diverging into separate but parallel routes, as if the waggoners grew weary of following the same ruts and struck out for themselves.

Then suddenly the mighty artery will be pinched into a single lane to cross a narrow bridge, built of wooden scaffolding. The only example of bridge-building that I saw along the way was entirely manned, if I may use the expression, by women. For some reason Russian women have a monopoly of road-making, and they are to be seen until late at night, in all parts of the country, digging ditches, mixing the tar, and trundling the steam-rollers.

Occasionally, we jolted through a small Ukrainian village, but seldom were we allowed to stop. Once, pleading thirst, we induced our local guide to permit us to drink at a village pump. At once we were surrounded by villagers, who wanted to examine our cameras, ball-point pens, and wrist-watches. Some members of the group apparently received tempting offers for their foot-wear, but we were speedily bundled back into the bus before any such transactions took place!

From the bus, the countryside had a curiously wild, unkempt appearance. The absence of fences accounts, perhaps, for some of this—since, presumably, it is unnecessary to mark off individual holdings in a country where private ownership does not exist. Milking shelters and overnight holding pens could be seen in the fields, however, near the clusters of farm buildings.

What contributed to the impression of wildness most of all was the profusion of weeds in the ditches and even among the rows of crops themselves. No attempt at weed-control, either by sprays or by mechanical cultivation, seemed to be made, except for the forlorn groups of white-kerchiefed women, fighting a losing battle on hands and knees among the corn.

The collective that was chosen for us to see was a farm of 8,500 acres, called the Twentieth Party Congress Farm, Odessa District. It was evidently an important centre, for the president of the collective, Makar Posnitny, is a Deputy to the Supreme Soviet, or Parliament.

The son of the president met us on arrival and took us out to see the farm. It was a pleasant-looking village of white-washed houses, set back from the street behind high walls and rather untidy gardens, with many flowers. Nature was apparently deeply loved, but not tended.

The houses of the farmers were all congested in a single street, called Peace Street—a dirt road, but with paved sidewalks. We were told each farmer owns his own home, receiving a building loan of five thousand roubles (five hundred dollars) from the collective, which he pays back over twenty years. He can also keep the produce of his own plot (about one and a quarter acres) for himself. Some of the houses had TV aerials on the roofs, but there appeared to be no running water.

At the bakery we watched the heavy, round loaves of bread being made. The bakery door was locked when we arrived and was opened from the outside by our guide with a key, although there were workers inside. It was also locked when we left, again from the outside. One of those many little puzzles for which there is no ready answer.

We called at the power plant—and noted that the generator was made by General Electric, Schenectady, N.Y. The cattle were fed in open-side stalls, which showed charts above each cow giving output per day (average reading: 15 kilograms). We asked if the milk was pasteurized and were assured it was, but we never did get to see the pasteurization plant.

On the whole, it appeared to be a prosperous, well-run farm, and it was remarkable to think that it had been twice burned to the ground, once by the anti-collectives in the thirties and again by the Germans in the Second World War. Like much in Russia today, it is a testimony to the tenacity of the Russian people.

The most lasting impression, however, was the general air of lifelessness, probably due to the absence of any mechanical equipment, or even any private cars. We saw no gas station in the village. We were informed that last year the collective spent $70,000 on equipment, including five silage combines, three corn harvesters, caterpillar and wheel tractors, etc. However, like the pasteurization plant, none of these were to be seen.

Another impression was the superfluity of people in the collective, compared to the amount of land. We were told that there were 1,500 people on this farm of 8,500 acres—almost one person to every five acres. Of these, 714—a figure that apparently included women and children—were working farmers.

The incomes of these people must be very restricted. The produce of the collective farm is all taken over by the Government, at a price that the Government determines, except for a small, variable residue, which is now allowed to be sold at free-market prices. How much does the individual farmer make?

He is, of course, allowed to keep the profit from his pathetically small plot, the produce of which may also be sold on the free market. Most of this would be required to support his own family, however, leaving little or none for sale. The figures we were given of total farm profit, less operating expenses, capital costs, and 10 per cent taken by the ministry, suggest that most farm families cannot hope to realize more than about $100 a year.

And if such people desire to seek a way out of the slavery and hopelessness of this life—what avenues of escape are open to them? Who will pay their expenses? Where can they go? No answers seemed to be obtainable to these questions.

For four hours, without any lunch, we took in the sights. Finally at 4:00 PM we came to the community hall, where a long table had been spread with endless plates of chicken, ducks, veal, ham, eggs, salad, fruit—all washed down with cider wine. We ate a full meal, then the waitresses cleaned the cloth and spread it all over again with more of the same.

The president, an earthy Khrushchov type of farmer, made an amusing speech. He told how he had been on a farm delegation to the United States. When he visited a farm near Washington, he said, he was given only a doughnut and a cup of coffee. We all felt duly impressed with the superiority of Ukrainian hospitality.

When we left, gifts of flowers and wine were handed in the windows of the bus. Everyone was deeply touched. It was only by chance, on the way ahead, that I learned from our guide that the banquet had been paid for out of Intourist coupons, so we had been regaled at our own expense!

Odessa is a pleasant, sleepy-looking city on the Black Sea. From my hotel window, I caught my first glimpse of the "wine-dark" sea sailed by Odysseus, after whom the city is named. What's in a name? Spoil-sports will assert that Homer's legendary hero never passed the Dardanelles at all into the Black Sea, but sailed westward, through the Pillars of Hercules (Gibraltar) into the Atlantic.

It is nevertheless a joy to make even so slight a contact with the Western ethos, here in the depths of the Slavic hinterland. I made a mental salutation to the memory of the great voyager, who sought the Happy Isles even, it may be, on this barbarous shore.

There is more than a touch of the Mediterranean world about this coast, which sweeps dramatically down, over long brown cliffs, broken by many inviting coves and sandy beaches, to the sea. The character of the people and the life, too, is touched with the romantic spirit.

In these old-fashioned cobble-stoned streets, you will meet Jews, Greeks, Armenians, Turks and Tatars, as well as Russians and Ukrainians. Odessa was once a thriving trade mart between Europe and Asia. But trade languishes under Communism, and the city now looks rather like a period clock run down, still telling the time of another era.

Today Odessa is chiefly remarkable for the number of pretty girls—a rarity in the Soviet Union. On the broad beaches there are many bikini-clad beauties to be seen. Where do they go when they go back to town? Presumably, they disappear into those sack-like garments that Soviet custom decrees for its puritanical womanhood.

The Intourist hotel is a solid structure of the czarist period, built around a small courtyard, shaded by giant trees. A central fountain decorated by Cupids drips water over moss-covered stones. Tables covered with white cloths are set in the open for dinner, served by an elderly waiter, so decrepit that he can hardly totter, but with all the grace and courtesy one misses in the Soviet world.

No doubt he is dismissed as a "bourgeois survival" (in the official jargon) by the bright young Communists of today. Why is it that all the best things in the Soviet world seem to me to be survivals of one kind or another? It is taken for granted today that a customer can wait interminably for his soup, stand in line for half an hour to get his stamps, be told to come back innumerable times to collect his passport at the hotel desk, and be shouted at if he dares, however timidly, to complain.

Perhaps I, too, am a survival, soon to be swept away by the march of progress. But I was grateful to this old man for his unfailing courtesy, which made me feel a little more at home in this inclement world.

This former resort city of imperial Russia also boasts an ornate and elegant opera house. A local ballet company was performing *Aladdin and His Wonderful Lamp,* which was billed as a new ballet, with original music and choreography. I bought a ticket.

What I saw was a magnificent product of State-subsidized Soviet culture, a stupendous production that literally groaned under the realistic settings, spectacular effects and a cast of several hundred. The wonderful lamp produced a genie five times life size out of a cloud of smoke. And Aladdin flew away into the wings mounted on a real flying carpet.

The ballet seemed nearer to music-hall or pantomime than it did to an art form. One is puzzled to account for such a lavish expenditure by the Ministry of Culture on a production that was not, in fact, art at all. Perhaps the object is propaganda rather than culture, after all.

Nothing would seem farther from Marxism than the *One Thousand and One Nights!* Yet, perhaps inevitably, Aladdin emerges on the stage of the Odessa Opera House as a full-fledged proletarian hero. When threatened with death by the Sultan, he is rescued by a revolt of the people, who slay the Sultan and hail Aladdin as their leader.

Yet one last thought is inescapable. Odessa, a provincial city of about 670,000 people, maintains a full-time ballet company, performing fifty weeks a year. Out of this single company comes a constant succession of new ballets, with original music, choreography and staging—and this is being repeated in every city of comparable size in the Soviet Union. Can we match it, or come close to it?

7

THE BLACK SEA COAST

Aboard a Soviet ship;
Yalta and the conference; memories of Chekhov;
shopping on the esplanade;
little children learn to love Lenin; a cab driver's story;
Sochi: the workers' paradise, the sanatorium system

The Soviet motorship *Abkhazia*, 23,000 tons, gleamed spotlessly at her moorings in Odessa harbour. It was a fine afternoon. A smart breeze blowing off the Black Sea made the red flags, emblazoned with the hammer and sickle, stand out from the ship's mast. The scene, with all the hurry to and fro on the dock, as cranes loaded heavy luggage and even private automobiles aboard, seemed ideally suited for a snapshot.

Apparently, Soviet authorities thought otherwise. Tamara, our interpreter, shepherded her flock up the gangway with stern injunctions to put our cameras away. It was only later, from the deck, that I spotted a flotilla of a least twenty camouflaged submarines alongside. Several cruisers of the Soviet fleet also patrolled the harbour. While signs of military preparedness are few in the Soviet Union, it is remarkable how greatly the eye of the camera is feared.

Porters carried our luggage up after us on their backs, two or three bags strapped together at a time, with the strap passed around the man's forehead like a coal heaver's. After hauling sixty pieces of luggage, our porter looked all in. Although tipping is officially scorned in the Soviet Union, I reached into my pocket. I found only a U.S. dollar, which could not be changed until the ship's office opened. Such currency can be changed at great advantage on the black market, however, so I slipped the porter the dollar. He took it gladly. There was nobody else in my stateroom at the time. About an hour later, after the ship sailed, Tamara gave me the dollar back without comment. How she came by it, who had seen the incident, and what happened to the porter remained a mystery.

The *Abkhazia* was an excellent ship, with comfortable staterooms and solid, well-appointed fittings. The name is that of one of the Autonomous Soviet Republics in the Caucasus. It is perhaps a little misleading, however, as I found a name-plate engraved "*Maria Theresa*, Bremen" in the boiler-room. The ship was probably part of Germany's war reparations.

First-class staterooms contained a bed, desk and chair, washbasin and closet—it was more luxury than we had enjoyed in most hotels in the Soviet Union. It was a little disconcerting, however, to find a different class of passengers preparing to spend the night on deck, right outside my porthole. Actually there appeared to be five classes of passengers aboard. There were first and second-class staterooms (second-class had four bunks); third-class passengers slept in dormitories in the hold, fourth-class were accommodated on the floor of the companionways, and fifth-class on the open deck.

The sharp division in the classes is one of the anomalies of the so-called classless society. All tourists are divided into five classes, each with separate quarters, dining-rooms and lounges, strictly graded according to category. This, of course, occurs in Western countries, where accommodation varies according to cost—one may patronize expensive or inexpensive establishments. But in the Soviet Union, where the State operates all facilities, the differentiation is much more marked.

One of the distinguished passengers on board was Ho Chi Minh, President of Communist North Viet Nam. He was apparently travelling *first* first class, as the entire corridor leading to his suite was cordoned off and guarded by Vietnamese and Russian soldiers. Through the captain, I endeavoured to arrange an interview, but without success. His reticence was more understandable a month later. It was immediately following this private visit to the Soviet Union that North Vietnamese forces began their abortive invasion of Laos.

I spent a good deal of time on the bridge with the captain, whose company I enjoyed. He had sailed abroad in many foreign ports and some of the flavour of other lands had rubbed off on him. He also handled his ship with great skill, negotiating several narrow and difficult harbours without the aid of tugs and without once scratching the paint. How does it happen, I wondered, that such examples of efficiency occur when the general operation of the country often appears haphazard in the extreme?

As we docked at Yalta, I watched crates unloaded from the ship, each with the international "wine-glass" code clearly printed on its side, to show which side is up—and every one had the wine-glass upside down. Throughout the voyage the ship's washrooms and toilets were allowed to become cluttered and smelly. There was no soap and no toilet paper. The plugs in the basin didn't fit. And yet the captain displayed feats of seamanship utterly unexpected!

Ah, Russia! Nation of *moujiks* and *sputniks!*

Yalta evokes memories. A little town of winding streets, climbing steeply from the water-front into the dark hills, the air smelling sweetly of oleander, myrtle and mimosa, the sea glittering far below. Is it possible that the fate of the world was settled here only fifteen years ago?

One of our excursions was to the Vorontzov Palace, about five miles out of town, along the rocky coast. It was here, in 1945, that Prime Minister Churchill stayed, while attending the Crimea Conference with President Roosevelt and Marshal Stalin

The palace was built by a Russian princeling in the early years of the nineteenth century. It is a curious structure, half Gothic, half Moorish, but reminiscent of nothing so much as one of those exotic fantasies built by the prosperous merchant class in many an unexpected corner of the English countryside.

Then the explanation was given by our guide. Prince Vorontzov was Imperial Ambassador to the Court of St. James's. At once I recognized another English characteristic—the excellent workmanship, so unusual in Russia. The smooth-cut stone, the solid panelling, the perfect groining—all came from England. Even the portraits in oils on either side of the fireplace are those of the Herbert family, of Wilton House near Salisbury, whose daughter Prince Vorontzov had married.

Churchill must have felt unexpectedly at home here. He describes the place vividly in his book, *The Second World War*: "Behind the villa rose the mountains, covered with snow, culminating in the highest peak in the Crimea. Before us lay the dark expanse of the Black Sea, severe but still agreeable even at this time of the year. Carved white lions guarded the entrance to the house and beyond the courtyard lay a fine park with sub-tropical plants and cypresses."

Churchill's stay was marked by several curious episodes. His Russian hosts were nothing if not hospitable. He had only to comment on the absence of fish in the fish-pond to have a whole shipment of rare specimens imported by air from far away. On another occasion, one of his staff remarked casually that there was no lemon peel in the cocktails. The very next day a lemon tree, loaded with fruit, was growing in the hall.

The receptions, the parties, the clinking of glasses in the grand hall, symbolized the "spirit of Yalta", which it was hoped would inaugurate a new era of peace and friendship among the great powers of the world. What happened to that dream in the post-war period is now a matter of history.

And it is one of the mysteries of history how the Western Allies came, in the rosy glow of victory and champagne, to sign away the destiny of a score of nations and half a billion people. At Yalta, Russia secured Estonia, Latvia, Lithuania, Poland, Czechoslovakia, Hungary, Rumania, Bulgaria, Yugoslavia, Albania, East Germany, Manchuria, Mongolia, Sinkiang, North Korea, the Kurile Islands and half of Sakhalin Island, for the Communist bloc. Thus Communism spread its boundries over four-fifths of the land mass of Europe and Asia.

In return, of course, Russia made some concessions. Free elections were promised in Poland, in deference to Churchill's insistence that the sovereign independence of Poland was to be maintained. "The Poles will have their future in their own hands," Churchill reported to Parliament. In fact, it was two years before the provisional Polish Government recognized by the Big Three held its elections (January, 1947). The results were rigged by the Communists. Washington and London denounced them and U.S. Ambassador Arthur Bliss Lane resigned in protest. But then it was too late.

Likewise in Asia. Russia recognized China's sovereignty over Manchuria and promised Generalissimo Chiang Kai-shek military and economic aid. Instead, over the next four years, the Soviet Union blocked the Nationalist Chinese return to Manchuria, aided and abetted the Chinese Communists, and looted Manchuria of twenty-six billion dollars' worth of industries.

The mystery of this Yalta conference, with its subsequent travesty of human justice, and the roles of the principal players —the enigmatic Stalin, the optimistic Churchill, and the dying Roosevelt, shadowed by the ambiguous figure of the American adviser Alger Hiss—will perhaps never be satisfactorily explained.

The easiest thing to say is that everyone recognized the importance of peace and friendship with Russia, and belief in Russia's good faith was the only rock on which a peaceful world could be constructed. Churchill commented later: "Our hopeful assumptions were soon to be falsified. Still, they were the only ones possible at the time."

Meanwhile, each generation breaks its head anew on the same problem, which has become the overriding problem for

all men of goodwill: can we ever have an understanding with
the Russians? Travelling through the Soviet Union in 1959, and
often called upon to raise my glass at dinner tables to "peace
and friendship", so fervently desired by all, I was reminded of
a letter written by Maj. Gen. John R. Deane, head of the U.S.
Military Mission to Moscow in 1945, to General George Mar-
shall:

> I have sat at innumerable Russian banquets and become
> gradually nauseated by Russian food, vodka and pro-
> testations of friendship. . . It is amazing how these toasts
> go down past the tongues in cheeks. . . . The party of the
> second part is either a shrewd trader to be admired or a
> sucker to be despised. . . . We must be tougher if we are
> to gain their respect and to work with them in the
> future.

This letter was forwarded to Roosevelt a month before Yalta.
He read it, and dropped it in the basket.

Another winding road in Yalta leads to the little Swiss-style
chalet where Anton Chekhov lived. The great Russian writer,
who seems more akin to Western minds than any other in Slavic
literature, came to the Crimea for his health at the turn of the
century. He was already a dying man, suffering from the tuberculosis that ended his life in 1904.

But his tireless energy, which produced an endless succession of plays, short stories and articles, has also left its mark
on this pleasant little health resort. Again the past seems near.
His housekeeper told me that Chekhov's sister lived in this
house until her death last year. And his fruit trees are thriving.
"Anton spent an hour every morning before breakfast plant-
ing and tending them," said the housekeeper.

Not that his sister, Mary, was pleased with the site at first.
Her first reaction was to burst into tears. The house he
selected had a picturesque view of the sea and the mountains,

but there were few advantages from a woman's point of view. It was a twenty-minute walk from Yalta, next to a Tatar cemetery, with no sewage or water supply, and overgrown with wild vines.

Chekhov's genius for creating something beautiful out of ugliness is reflected, however, in this house. He built a small square tower, terraces, and a glass verandah in a most unusual design. He planted a hundred rose bushes, and mimosa, cypresses, camelias, palms, figs, and eucalypti.

It was a pleasant household, filled with the coming and going of countless visitors, actors and actresses, writers, and pet animals of every kind. Chekhov had a pet crane that followed him like a shadow, flapping its clipped wings and performing its characteristic crane dance to the amusement of guests. This most compassionate of authors could not kill a living thing— even a wild dog was allowed to make its home under a tree in the garden. He used to catch mice as a hobby and then release them some distance away on the outskirts of town.

Nor did Chekhov content himself with improving his own property. He threw himself into the life of the town. He became governor of a girls' high school. He campaigned for better local government. A Chekhov cult grew up in Yalta which has not yet died out. He was much sought after by the opposite sex, so that a name—Antonoviki—was coined for these female admirers. Antonovki is also the name for a Russian brand of apples, so it has been translated as "Anton's pippins".

But the chief cause to which he devoted himself was the care of the sick. Tubercular patients were flocking to Yalta, often living in desperate poverty and in need of medical assistance. Chekhov organized a subscription all over Russia and impoverished himself to build and equip a tuberculosis sanatorium. Today the State takes good care of such patients, commented our guide with complacency.

Although Chekhov is now regarded benevolently by the State as a forerunner of the Revolution—his books deal mostly with characters from the lower depths—none of his writings in Russian were available at any of the book stores in Yalta— only technical works and text-books of Marxism-Leninism.

Shopping along the esplanade at Yalta also revealed the extreme dearth of novelties in the Soviet Union. It is not only that there were few things to buy, but they were the same things I had already seen in Moscow, Leningrad, Kiev and Odessa. The best of these were the small enamelled cups and saucers, and spoons—priced at sixty dollars for a cup and saucer, eight dollars and up for a spoon. It is interesting to speculate how many people can buy these trinkets in a society where the average wage is sixty dollars a month.

In the more reasonable price range, there were a few vases, with portraits of Tolstoy, Pushkin, and other Russian greats on them. Since I had not been able to find a single book by Chekhov, it occurred to me I might get his portrait in Yalta. But no, I was told the portrait-vases were all standard and did not include the local luminary. There were no local products, not even a souvenir with the word "Yalta" on it.

This extraordinary degree of standarization extends to all kinds of goods. The clocks, chandeliers, or china of Soviet manufacture in the hotels are all exactly alike. The favourite glassware pattern, for instance, is a sort of basket-weave design that adorned every tumbler and wine-glass I drank out of from Moscow to Tashkent. The sheer monotony would kill an ox with boredom.

Yet this is the natural outcome of state ownership of the points of production. All labour is drafted into the government factories. No one is left to carry on the local arts and crafts indigenous to each locality. The result is the annihilation of all regional character and individuality.

Along the esplanade, I caught the stern eye of Lenin upon me, looking down from his standard pedestal in the main square. "Great is the State," he seemed to say. "Thou shalt have no other gods but me."

Protracted negotiations with the Intourist office produced the promise of an interesting programme in Yalta, including visits to two sanatoria and a medical-research laboratory. As usual, most of this came to nothing; but, after much persistence, I was taken one morning to a children's sanatorium on the outskirts of the city.

It was set in a charming, old-fashioned park, small but pictur-esque, overlooking the sea. The road lay between giant pines, bordered by flowering shubs. The main building was a villa belonging to a lady relative of the late czar. It had been taken over by the State as a rest centre for juvenile cases of liver, kid-ney, and other internal illnesses.

We were met on the front steps by the medical doctor in charge, with a ready, open-handed gesture of goodwill. He was a man of forty, with a wooden leg and a smile of infectious happiness. I learned later that he had been a tank commander during the war. His one ambition now seemed to be to bring happiness to his large "family" of children.

We were immediately given white caps and enveloped in voluminous white gowns, for our tour of the establishment. The main building and several of the "summer houses" had been converted into wards and therapy units. The walks between were filled with flower beds and little fountains, and a flight of stairs led down to a private beach.

The equipment, which included a "sun" room of quartz lamps, was rather scarce and primitive. It was plain that re-sources were limited, but the best use was made of sun and air. The beds of the most serious cases were placed on an enclosed verandah, overlooking the sea.

Everywhere we went, the cheerful doctor was surrounded by his young flock, clinging to the tail of his gown with that pecu-liarly trustful look of the sick child. His was a lifetime mission of goodwill—which, he said, "our Soviet power has made pos-sible."

The sanatorium was operated by the Ministry of Health and each child was sent here at State expense, after being recommended by a medical board provided by the parents' trade union. It certainly represents one of the best features of the Soviet system.

On another occasion we visited a Young Pioneer Camp. The Young Pioneers are a Soviet equivalent of Boy Scouts and Girl Guides—but co-educational. The camp was located in a pleasant pine forest. My first reaction was one of relief—a sense of respite from the endless pressures of ideology, a retreat into nature that knows not Marx or Capital.

We came to a rustic gateway, decorated with flags. Inside were clusters of cottages and playgrounds, filled with children wearing the red kerchief of the Pioneers around their necks. The children, ranging in age from seven to fourteen, were organized in well-ordered groups, just so many to each activity, on the swings and see-saws. As we came by, each group broke off playing to bid us welcome.

Then, an almost uncanny thing. As we passed through the trees, each group broke into song, usually accompanied by a concertina, passing the song along from group to group as we appeared in view. Would any other children in the world, I wonder, behave in a like manner?

Along the way, signs and banners, usually not more then ten yards apart, lined the path. They bore such slogans as: "All hail to Lenin, founder of the Soviet State!" One interesting avenue was dedicated to countries friendly to the Soviet Union. The flags of all the satellite nations were there, of course, also China—and, rather surprisingly, France and Italy. But not Canada or the United States.

The children were extremely friendly and curious. Some spoke a little English and clustered around to look at our cameras and ball-point pens. What did they learn in their Pioneer camp? "We learn about Lenin, where he was born, where he lived, his activity in the Revolution, and his love for children."

We were invited inside an assembly hall to receive a briefing. A camp leader, a woman, told us there were 2,400 children in this camp, supervised by thirty team leaders and thirty teachers. A team leader is a student who organizes the games. A teacher is a graduate of an educational school whose duty is to guide the training. The camp appeared to be understaffed by our standards, yet there was no lack of discipline.

The main object of these camps, the leader said, is to give youngsters healthy bodies, and also to inculcate something useful: dramatics, crafts, music (a loud drum-and-trumpet ensemble outside testified to the latter effort) and, of course, "a daily lesson in world events".

I asked if the lesson for today could be produced, but was informed that there was no lesson that particular day. I had to be content with asking whether the interpretation of world events was given by the teacher independently, or dictated by higher authority. The answer: "It is dictated by higher authority."

There is no question that these children are healthy and well cared for. On the other hand, they do not appear to play with any abandon. Their movements are noticeably slow and deliberate, their speech has a rehearsed quality. I never witnessed a single squabble or fight.

The State has complete control over the lives of young people, from the nurseries (where they are called "Young Octobrists", after the revolution of October, 1917), through the school years (when they are "Young Pioneers"), to young adulthood (when they are enrolled in the "Komsomol Youth League").

It is no wonder that political indoctrination strikes deep roots. The surprising thing is the ability of the human mind to immunize itself to such massive doses of political virus. The educational commissars must be constantly surprised at the way their quarry ultimately escapes them.

I left the camp in the woods with some misgivings—glad now to return to the humdrum of ordinary life. Back in Yalta, I was relieved somehow to see, when looking about me, that Soviet children do grow up into ordinary, normal people after all.

About this time, some members of my group began to tire of the political indoctrination themselves. Instead of a constant round of statues of Lenin and museums of the Revolution, they wanted to enjoy themselves. And so they conceived the idea of driving to the top of the nearby mountain that overlooked Yalta.

At first they were informed this was impossible. The road, said the Intourist Guide, was obstructed due to landslides, also the surface had "melted in the sun". But the errant members of the party piled into a taxi one morning and persuaded the driver (with the aid of a tip) to lose the rest of the group, who were in vehicles up ahead. Instead of following the prescribed route, they headed up the mountain.

The road was perfectly clear and in good condition, and soon they reached the top, where there was a glorious view and a welcome chalet for refresment. Inviting the cab driver inside, they sat down and ordered tea.

But the driver was nervous. Perhaps he was afraid of the consequences of his act, or else he had something on his mind. Engaged in conversation by Israel Ginsburg, one of the Russian-speaking members of our group, he replied nothing at first; then two great tears welled up in his eyes and ran down his face.

Getting up, he ran outside, followed by Mr. Ginsburg. The man was sobbing like a child, his body shaking in convulsions as he leaned against a tree. When he regained control of himself, he told his story. He had a wife and four children, and his wife was too ill to work. Although medical expenses were paid for by the Government, she could not contribute to the upkeep of the family. As a cab driver he earned sixty dollars a month. It takes at least forty dollars a month to feed each person in a family, he explained. Consequently, there was not enough food for his children. They lived on black bread and bones.

Yet this man's superior in the taxi office, he said, made many times his salary and lived well. Nor was there any chance of advancement—although still a young man, he could not hope to better himself. "There is no hope for me," he concluded.

Every society has its inequalities and produces its unfortunates and its misfits. I do not know in which category the cab driver belonged; but it seemed a strange encounter in the country that claims to have abolished want and to have established social justice for all.

The matter of false information given by the Intourist guide also puzzled me. What was the purpose of misrepresenting the condition of the road, since this chance encounter could not have been foreseen? What, indeed, was behind any of the mystification that beset us in the Soviet Union? For this was not an isolated experience. It happened again and again, as anyone knows who has spent any time in this country.

During our stay in Yalta, I was a witness to an unseemly incident in which a youthful American tourist was involved. I chanced to enter the Intourist office at the hotel while this young man was creating a scene by pounding on the desk and shouting in a hysterical manner: "You have told me another lie—do you know what that means—L-I-E?" I must say the Intourist staff kept *their* tempers admirably, and the matter, which apparently was merely a question of accommodation, was eventually adjusted amicably enough. But I understood only too well the pressure that provoked the outburst.

It does something to us. It brings us into a suspicious, doubting frame of mind; it makes us disbelieve *everything*. This is a pity, because there is, of course, much to admire in the Soviet Union, as there is everywhere. But when we are worked upon by this constant mystification, we end up by being unable to recognize truth itself.

Further east, Sochi is the garden of the Black Sea coast. It loomed one morning out of my port-hole window, after an overnight voyage from Yalta. At first it was only a white dot on the shore, amid the luxuriant tropical vegetation. Above it the slopes of the Caucasian range rose in terraces, followed by densely wooded mountain ridges and snow-covered peaks.

Gradually the town took form and shape—the harbour with its fantastic administration building, like a Chinese pagoda with a red star atop; the stately sand-coloured palaces of the sanatoria, the bright red flowers of the formal gardens. Sochi, I was told, is the workers' paradise.

Going ashore, I found myself in a new city almost entirely built in the Soviet era. It was the first of this kind I had seen, and it looked truly elegant after so much shabbiness and decay. The main street, which followed the coast, was lined with magnificent brownstone palaces, set in splendid gardens and terraces, amid many fountains and a profusion of flowers. The street was linked with the beaches below by frequent cable cars.

The explanation for all this luxury is not far to seek. These are not private homes or commercial establishments; they are all public buildings, built by the Soviet Government as "Palaces of Culture and Rest". What the State has taken away from the worker with one hand, by giving him uniformly low wages, is returned in part with the other, in the form of free medical care and paid vacations.

Soviet citizens, riding on the buses and street-cars of Sochi, gawk and gape at the wonders of the workers' paradise. An increasing number, as time goes on, may begin to question the apportionment of the spoils and reckon up what they gain against what they lose to the State. Some may even resent the role of the State as arbiter in how the profit of their labour should be spent. But all must agree that Sochi is an island of beauty in the vast expanse of dreariness.

In Sochi, I paid a visit to the Metallurgists Sanatorium. A flight of 168 steps led up from the street to a central building, big enough for a state legislature, with gigantic Corinthian columns and neo-Greek architrave. The total cost of this edifice was said to be $6.7 million. There were 388 similar places along the coast, representing a total of $2½ billion worth of sanatoria.

The costs of hospitalization are borne 70 per cent by the State, 30 per cent by the patient. There was accommodation for 375 patients at the Metallurgists San, with a total turn-over of twelve or thirteen thousand patients a year. Hospital staff included two hundred technical personnel and ten doctors, of which seven were women.

The medical facilities available were considerably more modest than the grandiose architecture. Asked if any special vitamins were given for heart cases (the sanatorium specialized in cardiac lesions), the director said patients were given a nourishing drink made of wild roses. Otherwise treatment consisted entirely of sun and salt-water baths. I saw one deep-therapy unit and a half dozen basins with nose-douches, and that was all.

The philosophy behind such an institution is puzzling. What is the relation between the extravagant spending on architecture and the minimal cost of medical care? As a rest centre, the total medical and recuperative benefits of this hospital could be provided at one-thousandth part of the cost of this edifice.

A clue to this puzzle was given by the director of the sanatorium, Dr. Brezinsky. An imposing woman herself, fiftyish, with black hair (dyed) parted severely in the middle and tied up in a plait, the doctor is at once director, and secretary of the party organization in the sanatorium.

Her biography is revealing. She studied medicine for five years at Leningrad University on a scholarship. This scholarship paid for her tuition, lodging, books, clothes, everything. When she graduated, she was required, like all other students, to take a job assigned to her. She was sent to Sverdlovsk, where she studied a further two years at the University of Marxism-Leninism. These studies covered historical materialism, dialectical materialism, history of the Communist Party, and the works of Marx and Lenin.

I asked why she took this course and Dr. Brezinsky replied that Lenin said everyone, in every profession, is supposed to be politically educated. I asked if it meant bigger pay for her? Answer: No. A better post? Answer: No. However, upon graduating, she was appointed chief of the hospital at Sverdlovsk.

I asked what bearing her political training had on her present post. She replied that it gave her the right to control the administration of the hospital. Her role is not that of a doctor, she said, so much as an educator. I asked what proportion of her time was taken up with medicine and politics respectively. She replied that the State has decreed a 6½-hour working day for doctors, and this includes only medical work. The rest of her time is devoted to political activity.

Is the answer that the real purpose of all these sanatoria is political, like so much else in the Soviet Union, rather than medical? The psychological effect of all this grandeur on the minds of the four or five million persons funnelled through the sanatorium system every year is enormous. They may not be able to judge the medical benefit they receive, but they cannot but be impressed with the power of the State that houses them.

8

GEORGIA—STALIN'S LAST REDOUBT

In search of the Golden Fleece;
to Lake Ritsa; storm over the Caucasus;
Georgia in legend and history; the Stalin cult;
new and old Tbilisi; the man in the striped pajamas;
police break up a meeting; hunting for ikons;
aboard an Ilyushin-14

"And the word of the Lord came unto me, saying, Son of man, set thy face against Gog, the land of Magog. . ." (Ezekiel, 38) And so I did, setting forth, in an open charabanc full of tourists, from Sochi on the mountain road that leads to Lake Ritsa.

Soon we were among the high, shining mountains that divide Europe from Asia—a mighty wall, which to the ancients represented the end of the known world. Beyond lay the fabled lands of the Hyperboreans, the Gog and Magog of the Old Testament.

When Jason, that earliest traveller to these shores, landed here he found a Bronze-age civilization already flourishing. The Kingdom of Æa, whose riches amazed the rough-and-ready crew of the *Argo,* was also the land of the Golden Fleece. Supposed to be the fleece of a divine ram, stolen by the wicked king of the Æetes, the Fleece has been the subject of immense speculation.

Strabo, the ancient Greek writer, provides the most prosaic explanation. The sheep, he observes, rambling through the westward-flowing mountain streams of the Caucasus, picked up small particles of alluvial gold in their wool. Such a skin was offered by the crafty Æetes to Jason, who took it home with him to Greece.

Our road climbed upward from the coast, through breathtaking gorges, wooded to the heights and filled with the roar of mountain torrents. I looked with a certain fascination for the flocks of the Æetes, with their traces of gold, but saw none. Except for a few bee-keepers in the valleys, these mountains were lonely and lorn.

Far from any sign of human habitation, this is the last refuge of the romantic spirit. Here, in the literature of the nineteenth century, the ideal figure of the "world wanderer" sought his goal, the perfect union of Man and Nature, the peace of the Mind Eternal. Childe Harold might be startled, however, by the marks of others who have been here. Pompey came this way and, after an unsuccessful campaign, left his name and the number of his legion carved high on a rock. There is less grandeur in the graffiti of lesser men—such as "Paul Robeson was here" (in Russian characters).

We stopped along the way at a forest pool, reputed to be a fountain of youth that washes away the years. Several charabancs of tourists were drawn up alongside, while the occupants scrambled over the rocks and knelt down to wash their faces in the stream. The most eager participants in this ancient superstition were the Americans, while their Russian guides looked on with smiles of enlightened superiority. I washed my face unashamed, however. The water was cool after a hot drive and it did not matter that no wrinkles were removed.

Lake Ritsa was reached after a four-hour drive, climbing steadily all the way. The snow-covered mountains swept down steeply into a small lake of emerald green. A log-cabin hotel offered welcome hospitality, with a restaurant built on piles right out over the water. The food was excellent, the drink cold, and the view unexampled.

We travelled no further into the mountain, however, since this was the end of the road. The onward journey was to be made by air. After relaxing, therefore, we returned down the mountain road—a somewhat unnerving experience, since the driver persisted in coasting around the hairpin bends with his engine off. This trick, presumably to save gas, is characteristic of Russian drivers everywhere in the country. I never found out who gains by it—the driver or the State. It is said there is a brisk trade, however, in black-market gas.

Along the way I chatted with some of the American tourists, including an agronomist, Frank O'Bryne of Lake Wales, Florida. He told me he had been invited to an experimental station in Sochi, where he was shown a tree with forty-two different kinds of fruit grafted on to it. It seemed typical of the Russians to be hard at work producing *"sputnik* fruit trees", while there is still no fruit juice available at the breakfast table!

We took off from Sochi airport in an IL-14 for Tbilisi, across the mountains to the east. A louring storm hung over the mountains and the plane followed the coast southward for about fifty miles, looking for the pass through which it was to fly, since the aircraft did not have the power to rise above the towering peaks.

The darkness grew more ominous and I was not looking forward to negotiating the narrow gorges in such an aircraft during an electrical storm. It was almost with relief, therefore, that I saw that the captain planned to descend for an unscheduled landing at Sukumi, near the Turkish border.

We made several passes over the field, while some women cowherds ran frantically back and forth, driving their cows out of the way, and then set down for a bumpy but safe landing. Several other planes were also parked in the field, presumably waiting for better weather. The airport building was a wooden shack, offering the facilities of a restaurant and an outdoor latrine.

A Chinese girl, in cap and apron, who spoke excellent English (she spoke five languages), served us with ice-cold champagne at three dollars a bottle. As a rule, this was the only drink that was always available *cold*. Refrigeration facilities may be limited. It seemed odd, however, that it was to be had at all in such a remote and fly-infested place. I doubt if champagne could be ordered in even some of the larger American airports. Apparently the best is always available for the few in the "classless society".

After a delay of some four hours, we took off again. It was now darker and even more louring than before, and no explanation was made to the passengers of the reasons for either the unscheduled stop or the departure. Some thought that military troop movements to the Turkish frontier might account for the delay.

No answer to this kind of speculation was ever forthcoming. In an effort to settle the matter, I asked the young woman who met us at Tbilisi, representing the Intourist office, if bad weather had prevailed over Tbilisi. "It never rains in Tbilisi," she replied off-handedly. I looked out the window; it was raining hard. I gave it up, thankful, at any rate, to have arrived safely.

The Caucasus is the traditional home of gods, heroes and brawlers. One after another they arose—Gog and Magog, Prometheus, Tamara the warrior queen of Georgia, whose rule ushered in a golden age. Tamara (1184-1212) ruled over a chivalrous and Christian kingdom of five millions. The architectural splendour of her churches and palaces rivalled the medieval glories of the Europe of her day. But within a few years of her death, all was to vanish before the annihilating onslaught of the Mongols.

Again and again, we encounter the enduring effects of this holocaust among the peoples of Eastern Europe and the Near East. We can only reflect on the good fortune of the countries of

Western Europe, which were spared this fate and allowed to develop in their own time and way.

Tamara, as a woman, left a rich lode of anecdote in the history of Georgia. A descendant of the Bagratid dynasty that ruled Georgia for twelve hundred years, she is immortalized by the Russian poet, Lermontov, as an eternal *femme fatale*.

Her rule was marked, however, by a rare respite in the long history of horror for which Georgia is renowned. She fought like a man, but spared her victims like a woman. Married as a girl to George Bogolyubskoi, an unscupulous adventurer, she subsequently divorced him. George, however, raised an army to recover his crown. "King for a day", he was soundly defeated and delivered up to Tamara. His fears may well be imagined.

Tamara's father, Giorgi III, had placed his rivals, the Orbeliani family, in a similar situation. After his victory, Giorgi III settled the dynastic issue in traditional Georgian fashion, with the blinding iron and the castration knife. (The whole seed of the Orbeliani was literally destroyed.)

George Bogolyubskoi must have been understandably apprehensive. Tamara, however, established a Georgian precedent by pardoning her erstwhile husband and banishing him to Byzantium. It is possible that Georgia might have become a polite and civilized nation. But less than four years after Tamara's death, couriers brought news to the Bagratid Court of the arrival of a "strange people, speaking a strange tongue". It was the Mongol horde. The Georgian Golden Age was at an end.

Blood feuds, massacres, and atrocities mark the remainder of Georgia's history. Many Georgians steadfastly refused to submit to the conquerors, Mongol or Russian. Among them were the Chechens, a race that considered itself composed exclusively of princes. Shamyl, King of the Chechens, was the last knight of chivalry. Tall, blue-eyed and handsome, he led a *jihad* (holy war) against the Russians in the last century. Tales of his prowess and escapes are part of the folk-lore of Georgia. He could jump over a trench twenty-seven feet wide. The best

Russian generals were sent against him and he defeated all in turn. Once he was trapped in his mountain stronghold. Although severely wounded, he escaped by jumping over the heads of the enemy and disappearing into the hills.

In 1854 the Crimean War broke out. Shamyl sought aid from the British and the Turks. But in the end he was all alone. Trapped in their eyrie, his band had diminished to four hundred men. They fought until only twelve remained. Shamyl surrendered. The Czar spared his life, but with his death in 1874, all hope of Georgian freedom disappeared.

The last of the god-heroes of Georgia was Stalin. Only against this background of his native Georgia is it possible to evaluate the despotism that Stalin imposed on the Soviet Union as a whole. Despite all the tergiversations of the Soviet propaganda machine, Stalin's diabolic role in history is not to be concealed. He seemed to regard it himself with a characteristic Georgian pride. The outspoken Lady Astor asked him once when he was going to stop killing people. He answered: "When it is no longer necessary." Churchill asked him during the Second World War how many *kulaks* he had liquidated. Stalin answered with extraordinary frankness: "Ten million. It took four years."

He was still at it when he died. And yet, despite the undisguised savagery of his reign, a Stalin cult grew up that raised him to the rank of a living god. It is hard to believe that in our time such cult-worship was ever enforced upon a great nation of two hundred million people. Fifteen towns, innumerable factories and streets, the highest peak in Russia, were named after him. A new metal was called Stalinite. An orchid was named Stalinchid. Children stood before their desks each morning and recited, "Thank you, Comrade Stalin, for our happy life." Newspapers, writers and poets addressed the man in phrases meant for God: "O Thou Mighty One, Chief of Peoples, Who callest man to life, Who awakened the earth to fruitfulness, O Sun, Who art reflected by millions of hearts. . ."

Perhaps the greatest secret of Khrushchov's popularity in the Soviet Union is the fact that he said what everyone else was afraid to say. His speech to the Twentieth Party Congress in 1956 was like the opening of a great sluice in a dam. Over and over I heard its echo in the words of ordinary men and women: "Stalin was a tyrant, a butcher, a murderer."

But not in Georgia. Here the native son is still acclaimed in the tones of god-worship. The denunciation before the Twentieth Party Congress provoked some ugly reaction in Tbilisi, the Georgian capital. Students marched, demanding the overthrow of Party Chairman Khrushchov, and the self-appointed liberator was forced to use some Stalin-type methods himself to crush the opposition.

Today Tbilisi slumbers peacefully, a city of terraces built into the surrounding hills, intersected by a maze of streets. The "new town" (mostly of the czarist period) has impressive boulevards, lined with trees and interspersed with squares. A massive red-stone presidium of Soviet construction, faced with rows of soaring arches, dominates the main street.

An aerial cable-car links the town with the top of a mountain near by, and crowds line up for many blocks to avail themselves of this escape from the stifling heat on summer nights. It operates efficiently and smoothly, though its small gondola is entirely inadequate to the clamouring demand.

The "old town", dating back to the times of Georgian independence, nestles in the valley beside the river. The streets are narrow and tortuous, flanked by three- and four-story wooden buildings, with balconies across the front of each floor, from which a Juliet might cast a flower or to which a Romeo might easily climb, if romance were in fashion in Tbilisi today.

Many of the buildings are dug into the hillside and are more like cave-dwellings than houses. Swill and refuse litter the streets. Poverty here is centuries old and shows little sign of loosening its grip on the Georgian people.

Yet when I penetrated these foul-smelling regions of the old town and knocked at doors to ask a direction, I was welcomed in and offered tea from the samovar. Not a trace of ill-will for the Westerners was discernible in these people, whose faces, often dark and Oriental in character, break into smiles of great hospitality at the sight of a foreigner.

The Intourist hotel, which belongs to czarist times, is a good example of the amenities of this resort today. Four stories high and without the service of an elevator, it provides accommodation that has earned it the name among Western visitors of "The Goat's Nest". A warren of rooms, many without bathrooms, toilet facilities or even wash-basins, it is entirely furnished with broken remnants of imperial grandeur.

There were, so far as I could discover, no theatre performances, concerts, sports or entertainment in Tbilisi during my stay. The heat was oppressive and the prospect of staying indoors uninviting. In the evenings, therefore, I joined the townsfolk in the custom of promenading up and down the broad, tree-lined pavement.

After several passes before the hotel, a small middle-aged man stopped me, asking in Russian for a light for his cigarette. *"Ya no govorio pa Ruski* (I speak no Russian)," I replied, adding that I was Canadian. I passed him my lighter. The man took a long draw on his cigarette and handed back the lighter. "I too am a Canadian," he said in a low voice.

Nothing could have seemed more unlikely. The shabby-looking individual before me was wearing the top of a pair of striped pyjamas, unpressed pants, cloth shoes and no socks. He followed my glance. "I *was* a Canadian," he explained apologetically. "My home is here now."

"Let's walk," I suggested. He told me he was born in Canada of Russian parentage. He had been a tailor's cutter in Hamilton, Ontario before World War II. During the Depression, times were bad. For months he had no work and stood at the soup kitchens waiting for a handout. Then he sold his share of the business and sailed to Russia with his wife.

In the Soviet Union he had no difficulty in finding work; skilled cutters were in considerable demand. But now he worked in a Government factory that employed about five hundred people. Sixty of the personnel were bosses of one kind or another, so production was poor. Working conditions, he said, were not only bad but were getting worse. Hourly rates had dropped sharply, so that now he had to work twelve hours a day to earn as much as he did last year in eight hours.

The tailor kept glancing from side to side as he talked, as though afraid he might be overheard. I suggested we might go up to my room in the hotel for more privacy. He agreed. But once inside, he appeared even more nervous and unwilling to speak above a whisper. Thinking I might really be compromising him, in my desire to learn about his life, I asked for his address and suggested I visit him later at home. He scribbled it on a bit of paper and got up to go.

When I opened the door, however, the entrance was blocked by the formidable figure of the woman on duty in the hall. Soviet hotels are constructed in such a way that the passages on each floor are all within view of a central desk, where someone keeps watch over all comings and goings, night and day. It is impossible to enter or leave one's room unobserved.

At the sight of the woman, who had obviously been spying at the door, the little tailor froze to the spot and I had to lead him past her. On the way downstairs we continued to be closely followed, and so I said good-bye to my new friend and turned back to block the way to the woman behind. However, she brushed passed me and succeeded in tracking the tailor out into the street for about one block, before he became lost in the crowds of strolling promenaders.

The next day, I set out to find the address he had given me. This was by no means easy. I did not dare to hire a taxi driver, who might report my movements. I did not know which direction to take on foot, and no map of the city streets was available in any book store.

I began by getting on a street-car—any street-car—and asking the conductor for the street I wanted. At first, no one had heard of it. Consultations among the passengers. Then it was decided I was going the wrong way and I was put on another street-car. The conductor of the first car spoke to the conductor of the second car, who took charge of me with enthusiasm. After that I was transferred to several other cars, the passengers in each taking a friendly and helpful interest in my case. All this without a word of Russian!

So at last I found my way to the given address. It was in an ill-smelling part of town, on a hill, that I had visited earlier. The houses or shacks were built into the side of the cliff and connected by a long covered verandah. Hens and chickens pecked about in the street. I was directed to a door at the end, where the little man in the striped pajamas met me.

He invited me into a small room, perfectly kept, clean, neat, and in good repair. The room contained two beds, a wardrobe, table and chairs. A kitchenette was concealed in a cupboard. There were lace curtains on the windows and family pictures on the wall. But it was painfully evident that the couple were in dire poverty. Conversation was still constrained, but enough was said to sketch a picture of their life.

The tailor earned $100 a month. He paid $10 rent. He said that to live decently and without excess, food for two persons should cost $150 a month. Since he doesn't earn so much, I asked how he managed. He indicated the answer by tightening his belt.

I asked if everyone else was living in similar circumstances. He answered, "Very many—all honest people." He added that many live by the black market, bribery, and other dubious means. But he would not talk politics.

I asked if things were better now than they had been in former times. He agreed. Then, he said, he would have been arrested if he had even come to speak to me in the street. There had been some nights when he was afraid to come home to sleep, lest he be picked up on some fancied suspicion and sent to Siberia. "Thank God," he said without irony, "we are now more free."

Meanwhile I continued with my curb-side meetings. Outside the hotel at eleven o'clock at night a crowd of a hundred or more would gather. It usually began with a simple question. A Russian student would ask if I spoke English. I would say "How is life?" The first answer was usually "Good!" Then we would begin to compare notes. Others would ask more questions, and the student would translate my replies.

They asked why our newspapers lie about the Soviet Union. "We want peace and friendship," they said. I replied by telling them we do, too. Then I explained our system of a free press, how we have newspapers that support the Government and others that oppose it. This surprised many people, but they usually agreed that it was a good idea.

Their information about world affairs was singularly limited. I met no one who knew the name of Prime Minister Diefenbaker. But many asked about our Communist leaders and could name several, starting with Tim Buck. I explained that the Communist Party is not forbidden in Canada but that it has not one elected member in our House of Commons. This caused general surprise. It is taken for granted that the Communist Party is a great force in the outside world. Such is the effect of propaganda.

They demanded to know how much the average worker earns in Canada. I replied by telling them how much a week's pay will buy in goods and services. In every case they agreed they are worse off. "But then we have our Seven-Year Plan!" Most people believe it is necessary to tighten their belts in order to build up the country, and that the new plan will solve all these difficulties in time.

When the question of rent came up, they said they were better off. Rent is very cheap in the Soviet Union, where the only landlord is the Government—it usually amounts to about 10 per cent of a man's pay. I replied that under the National Housing Act an ordinary Canadian city dweller may own his own house in twenty years or less, something quite impossible in Russia.

Inevitably, a good deal of the time was taken up with discussion of freedom. I explained that everyone in Canada enjoys complete freedom. Most people in the crowd replied that they, too, have freedom. For example, they believe they can criticize their Government whenever they like. And they do express strong criticisms of the bureaucracy, the inefficiency and corruption of officials. "But can you criticize Communism?" I asked. "No," they admitted, "but then we don't want to anyway."

The astonishing thing about these meetings was the freedom in which they were held. As a rule the police were in evidence, but did not interfere even to clear the street for traffic. But in Tbilisi things turned out differently.

After a debate of about one hour outside my hotel, the leader suddenly said: "Good-bye, we must go now." "Why?" I asked. He answered, "It is our custom." I was then grabbed from behind by a policeman, who led me towards the hotel entrance. About twenty other policemen with clubs broke up the meeting. There was bedlam for a moment. Even an old beggar woman, who had received a few kopecs and candy from tourists at the door, was seized by the police and carried off screaming. Then all was quiet again. Couples began strolling by as though nothing had happened.

In our idle moments, many of us indulged in pastimes such as ikon hunting. This pursuit, so popular with tourists in the Soviet Union, is complicated by the fact that, although the State officially condemns religion, all known ikons have been enumerated by the Government as national treasures and cannot be taken out of the country. So the game is to locate those that have escaped enumeration—in other words, those in private hands. Most inveterate ikon-hunter in our group was Fred Peel. He had a special knack for dropping into conversation with a priest who promised to open his secret store.

Ikons are small portraits of the Saviour or the saints, in which the vestments are actually made of beaten gold or silver, sometimes encrusted with gems. They are believed to derive from the portraits of mummies of Hellenistic Egypt, executed in tempera on wooden panels that were laid on the coffins. From the fourth century they were in great vogue in the Byzantine world. The ikon was essentially an artistic medium of the Byzantine mind —from the painted wooden panels of the poor to the exquisite masterpieces of the jeweller's art. The very special beauty of the Georgian ikons is in the complicated backgrounds, similar to the complicated carvings of the Georgian churches.

One evening, Fred Peel burst into my room at the hotel. "I am on to one—not one—dozens!" he exclaimed. He told me he had met a priest who had made an appointment to show him some secret ikons that very evening at the Sioni Cathedral, after the evening service. An hour later, we were both in the Orthodox Church as the service began.

The Sioni Cathedral, which dates from the reign of Tamara, is a "centralized" church of the Byzantine type; that is, it has a quadrangle designed to direct the gaze upward to the arched dome of the cupola, which with its painted frescoes represents the vault of heaven. The walls and even the pillars were hung with hundreds of dazzling ikons. Each was illuminated by a bank of lighted candles and glowed with burnished gold. It was easy to understand how, in the passing of centuries, the ikon had come to be venerated not only as a sacred picture, but as sacred in itself. Was it possible to purchase something sacred?

The Orthodox service lasts about two and a half hours. There is no sitting accommodation. We stood in the choir stall, in the body of the church. The choir consisted of the lay reader and two old men who sang the responses. There was something strangely moving about the perfunctory air with which these grey and shabby men rested against a stone pillar during the long celebration of mass, like ancient carved statues expressing grief and resignation, only to come to life at the precise moment required, with a beautifully modulated vocal response.

People came and went in the church, visiting the various ikons around the walls, prostrating themselves before each, kissing the stone floor, the walls, and the glass covering the ikon itself. An aged man knelt beside me, praying aloud, his eyes fixed on the face of a sloe-eyed Byzantine Madonna. His prayer was a conversation, accompanied by innumerable changes of expression and intonation, in which he alone heard the reply.

Finally the last kyrie was sung, the congregation departed and the candles were put out. The aged priest, with creaking shoes and a white mane and beard, approached us. We were looking for ikons? What would we like—Christus, Madonna, St. George . . . ?

We followed him with beating hearts. Taking a big bunch of keys, he opened a cupboard at the back of the church where the candles are sold. Reaching in, he took out a handful which he tossed on the table before us. "Take them," he said, smiling benignly.

They were only small, printed paper cards!

The airport at Tbilisi is a fine modern structure, like all public buildings in the Soviet Union—with marble halls, tall columns surmounted by an elaborate frieze, and a spiked tower topped by an illuminated star. It was built only four years ago. A visit to the rest-room, however, revealed only a row of holes in the floor, without seats or cubicles of any kind.

On the landing-field—a grass strip—our plane was being loaded for the return flight to Moscow. It was an Ilyushin-14. Seating accommodation was for only thirty, but at least half a dozen passengers were taken on in the freight compartment, in addition to our luggage, a full load of mail, and a truck-load of crates containing fruit, vegetables and chickens.

I asked the stewardess if we were not over weight. "Please be quiet!" she replied, with Olympian calm. No warm-up was made before take-off. None of the Russians fastened seat belts during take-off or landing, but walked about in the aisle and leaned over the backs of seats. The flight, however, was smooth and punctual.

Perhaps we are getting soft in North America!

CHAPTER

9

KAZAKHSTAN, A CLOSED AREA

Alma-Ata, an Asian Capital;
nocturnal adventures; the people of Soviet Asia;
a visit to the Kazakh Academy of Science;
the mystery of the forbidden factories; missiles, sputniks, and
the Soviet space programme;
the opening up of Soviet Asia; Mme Udolskaya, a Soviet
woman scientist

In Moscow I bade farewell to the group of Canadians who had accompanied me so far on my journey. They headed back to the grasshopper playgrounds of the decadent West, while I went on to explore the further reaches of the worker-ant civilization.

On the airfield in Moscow a dozen new Soviet jets stood proudly, gleaming white and sleek among the soiled, weather-beaten commercial aircraft of the Western air-lines. "How do you like our Soviet planes—better, eh?" enquired a Russian airport official. He sighed pityingly. "Yes, the West is very backward!"

The TU-104 is a magnificent aircraft. Carrying 110 passengers, it makes the flight from Moscow to Alma-Atta in Central Asia, a distance of about 2,400 miles, in just over four hours. I was a little disconcerted to find a rubber oxygen mask placed at my disposal, but it proved to be unnecessary as the pressurization inside the cabin, though low, was adequate.

Flying at a height of twenty thousand feet, we passed over the Urals—a range of hills surprisingly low, so that one wonders at the strategic value that has been placed on this barrier between Europe and Asia. Next comes the great plain or steppe. An area larger than all of Europe, it is as little known as the far side of the moon; and with good reason, since this entire plain is closed to foreigners.

Travel in the Soviet Union is complicated by a proliferation of closed areas—in which, however, there may be open cities. (On the other hand, there are many open areas in which there are closed cities.) One of these open cities is Alma-Ata, capital of the Soviet Republic of Kazakhstan and main staging area for air flights to the Far East.

No photographs may be taken, however, during flight or landing at Alma-Ata, or from any high building in the city, or from any height of land overlooking the plain. It is not permitted to leave the city without a special authorization, and visas to visit any other cities of the Kazakh Republic are impossible to obtain.

Alma-Ata nestles into the mountain range that forms the western extremity of China. It is a picturesque town, by Soviet standards, with wide streets and sidewalks separated from the roadway by rushing streams, and a double row of overhanging trees. The buildings, except for the ponderous Soviet-style presidium, opera house and other public edifices, are old merchants' houses with whitewashed walls and low, overhanging eaves, decorated with wooden fretwork, dating back to the days when this was a czarist trading post by the name Vernyi.

The Intourist hotel is a typical czarist bungalow, consisting of half a dozen small suites, suitably furnished with velvet curtains, plush chairs, and gold-fringed lampshades. The dining-room is filled with taciturn Russian air-force officers and Chinese-looking Kazakhs drinking bottled mare's milk. A provincial air pervades the town; the shops are few and contain almost nothing at all. It is hard to realize that this is a metropolis with a population listed at 330,000.

At night it is almost impossible to sleep for the continuous barking of large, savage dogs. Once, I got out of bed and decided to walk abroad. The streets were inadequately lit by an occasional street lamp, the light from which did not penetrate the overhanging trees. No citizens were about, but I was startled to encounter several armed men in greatcoats and stocking caps, carrying rifles and knives, who roughly ordered me on my way. I was even more disconcerted when I twice stumbled across a man's body, lying in the pathway, clutching a rifle.

I enquired about these nocturnal encounters, but the hotel officials expressed complete ignorance. Local citizens, however, told me that store-keepers and householders hired personal bodyguards to protect their property. I was not able to discover who the potential lawbreakers might be, and when I suggested the existence of guerilla bands in the hills my informants became extremely glassy-eyed and vague.

In the market-place of Alma-Ata, a pleasant surprise awaited me. The stalls, mostly open tables, were at this season piled high with fruit. The raspberries were especially large; the peaches, though not free-stone or as good in colour as ours, were very tasty; and the melons, a sort of honey-dew variety, were the most succulent I ever ate.

I was especially pleased to find all this fruit, since none ever seemed available at the hotels. This was probably accounted for by the extremely high prices—although $30 a day at the Intourist rate might seem to have warranted such delicacies. Yet business was brisk and customers lined up with bottles and baskets to carry away their purchases.

I found that no containers were supplied by the merchants, which created something of a problem. I set out on a vain search in the stores along the main street for a box or a paper bag. No such article being available, I returned to the market-place and filled my hat with fruit instead!

What an extraordinary mixture of people were in the market! Most of the merchants were Kazakhs—women with golden skins, full lips and delicately arched brows, wearing long-fringed shawls, cowl-like over the head and around the neck and shoulders. Their Chinese coat-dresses were of delicate colours, jade green, mauve, and cherry. Above all, their looks were so pleasant and serene. Even the menfolk, in their open-neck shirts and square Chinese skull-caps, were extraordinarily agreeable in appearance.

Among them, in almost equal numbers, were the Russian women, who wore European-style print dresses, and Russian men in floppy hats and baggy pants. And here one glimpses the secret of Soviet success in Asia—a complete integration of races. All these people, of vastly different backgrounds and outlook, are unified by one idea—Communism. While the conflict of forces and interests in the democratic world often serves to keep nations and peoples apart, the catalyst of Sovietization aims at uniting them in a common cause.

The Soviet people are very proud of this elimination of racial prejudice. They often laughed when I enquired whether there was any ill-feeling between races in schools or on the job. This cannot be, they assured me, because all have equal opportunity and because "under Socialism there is work for all."

But perhaps there is another side of the story. It should not escape notice that the emergent character of this integrated world is predominantly Russian. These are Russian buildings in Alma-Ata, the food in the hotels is Russian, the street signs are in Russian, the goods in the stores are Russian. Formerly there were three or four million Kazakhs living on these steppes. Today there are an equal number of Russians, and more are coming all the time. Soviet Asia is the only part of Asia where the white race is still colonizing.

One cannot help wondering if this will not lay the ground-work for friction in the future. With the emergence of China as the Communist giant in Asia, a reaction may set in, which will swing the Asian people of the Soviet empire away from Russia and toward China. This is a development which Russia should and undoubtedly does fear. The great struggle of the future may not be between Russia and the West for possession of Europe, but between Russia and China for possession of Asia.

Alma-Ata is the seat of the Central Asian development programme. And so one morning I called at the Kazakh Academy of Sciences, where I was received by a gentleman who introduced himself as the Director of Scientific Research of the Institute of Energy. A Kazakh, and rather a pompous individual, for some reason he was extremely reluctant about revealing his name. Our interview began like this:

"May I have your name, sir?"

"Have a glass of mineral water. It is very good. A local brand."

"Thank you, no. I didn't catch your name."

"I am sorry. I haven't a card."

"Could you spell your name for me?"

"I'll send the card to you later."

"I'd be glad to have the name now."

"You are welcome."

I asked Tamara to get his name but she omitted to do so. The card never came.

The director spoke at length about the development of this enormous land, lying directly north of the Himalayas, between the Caspian Sea and China. It is rich in natural resources; all minerals in the metallurgical table, he said, are found in Kazakhstan, including the world's highest production of chrome, as well as rion ore, copper, zinc, lead, etc. "All these deposits are used, of course, for the better living of our people."

Before the Revolution, the director continued, this was the most backward province of Russia's empire. Today it is one of the biggest industrial areas, not only in Asia but in Europe as well. None of its resources were known until developed "by Soviet power".

On the question of industrial capacity, he claimed that the production of electricity is today greater than anywhere else in

Asia—six billion kilowatt hours—"so that if you compare us with Japan, even Japan lags behind." By 1965, he assured me, hydro-electric power in Kazakhstan would be ahead of all capitalist countries, except the United States.

"And what is the product of all these industries?" I enquired.

"Have a glass of mineral water."

"It is a break," intervened the interpreter.

I poured the director a drink, and one each for Tamara and myself. A group of assistants, who sat on the sidelines without a word, followed suit. After a short colloquy in Russian, Tamara turned to me again.

"Now the director would like to ask you a question."

"Please."

"Why do you keep your Indians in Canada penned up like animals in a zoo?"

For the next fifteen minutes we discussed the superiority of the Soviet system of racial integration, whereby Kazakhs and Russians live and work in harmony, the superiority of Soviet economic justice which eliminates wasteful competition, the superiority of Soviet total planning down to the last detail for the benefit of all. Was not this superiority self-evident?

"We have a different philosophy," I answered.

"Philosophy is international," he said severely, "therefore there is only one correct philosophy which must prevail everywhere."

I felt a cold shiver.

Before leaving, however, I made one more attempt to elicit the information I wanted.

"What is the nature of the industrial products of Kazakhstan?" I asked.

There was a painful silence. Then the director replied slowly:

"I cannot tell you."

It seemed I had stumbled on a forbidden subject.

When flying over the vast territory of Kazakhstan, you can see more than a dozen large cities below, all obviously new, built in well-planned concentric rings around industrial plants, served by railway marshalling yards. Yet these cities are separated by thousands of miles from the most populous centres of the Soviet Union.

The Seven-Year Plan calls for the establishment of new industries which supply technical equipment for radio, electronics and astronautics. This is known to include the creation of "scientist cities", such as Novosibirsk (with basically physical-engineering specialization) and Irkutsk (with chemical-engineering specialization) and others, all of which are closed to foreigners.

These deserts are also known to be the launching ground of Soviet missiles. It was here in 1957 that the first Soviet *sputnik* was launched, and also in 1959 the spectacular moon satellites. Considering the immense problems of transportation, not to mention the secrecy involved in transporting rockets, either assembled or in parts, to the launching sites, it is likely that where these missiles are fired they are also being made.

If even a fraction of the industrial output of Kazakhstan were going into missiles, and if these figures for fantastic industrial development were even partly correct, then we might imagine that the Soviet missile programme is already very far advanced indeed.

The overwhelming impression of this forbidden Asian republic is that of an unknown, pent-up power, ready to burst upon the world some day. It is like a kingdom of the trolls, where the weapons of the gods are being forged. Let us hope they are weapons of peace.

I was taken to the astronomical observatory of Alma-Ata, where the first photographs were made of the Soviet *sputnik* in orbit. The road led upward into the Tien Shan hills, overlooking Alma-Ata. It was a rustic countryside, full of fruit orchards and gushing streams, under towering snow-capped peaks.

The silver domes of the observatory glinted in the sunlight

as we pulled up before the main building. We were received on the front steps by the Assistant Director, Professor Korimov— a youngish man, slight, earnest, bespectacled, and singularly free from restraint.

He led us into a circular chamber under the central dome, a plain whitewashed room, with photographs of heavenly bodies around the walls. The furnishings were spare and the displays of equipment were primitive. We were told, however, that this was one of the three best observatories in the Soviet Union.

Professor Korimov himself was frank and friendly. Obviously at home in his work and proud of the achievements of his profession, he represented the class of specialist that benefits most under the Soviet system. Completely absorbed in his work, he clearly cared little for comfort or financial reward, although his salary was probably far in excess of those of his fellow-workers in less sensitive professions in the Soviet system. He was also entirely non-political in his thinking and refused to discuss such matters.

As we took a stroll through the grounds to visit one of the giant photo-telescopes, he outlined the Soviet space programme to me. The two most immediate goals, he said, concerned the launching of guided and recoverable satellites, to be followed by manned vehicles. Lunar and planetary shots would be followed by the creation of interplanetary stations, on which a number of men could remain for some time. He thought the creation of such stations could be the starting-point for travel to Mars and Venus. "The time is not far off when we will change from artificial earth satellites to interplanetary rockets," he added.

This raised the question of the military significance of such a programme. Professor Korimov rejected the idea. Space stations would be unsuitable for earth surveillance, he said, since photo-telescopes could not photograph the earth from space as they can photograph the moon, due to the density of the earth's atmosphere.

I wish I could share Professor Korimov's enthusiam for space exploration and detachment from political considerations. For it seems evident that the Soviet space programme, if successful, amounts to Communism taking over the rest of the solar system. And, if that happens, how is Communism on earth to be contained?

At any rate, the Soviet Union is expected to retain its lead in space technology for many years. It is the great paradox of the age that the Soviet system has achieved such a commanding lead in the technology of space before it has answered the most basic needs of its own people.

On the outskirts of Alma-Ata a large red-painted propaganda sign reminds the citizens that before the days of Soviet power, this was a city of dust roads, camels and goats, people did not eat bread, and literacy was only 2 per cent. Today, the message proclaims proudly, it is a mighty metropolis, with 2 universities, 27 technical schools, 20 agricultural schools, 4 agricultural colleges, 11 scientific research institutes, 15 experimental stations. . . and one hundred per cent literacy.

On the university campus, I fell into conversation with a young student of physics. He spoke good English, was neat and better dressed than most. I asked what he was doing during the summer holidays. "Nothing," he answered nonchalantly. Could he afford to be idle? "Oh yes, we have plenty of money!"

His father was a professor in the university and earned $400 a month—a figure nearly ten times the average wage in this part of the Soviet Union. How many hours did his father put in at his job? "About four hours a day." Was this at all unusual? "Many people in the Soviet Union now earn much money for little work."

Education is the high road to success in the Soviet world today. The gap between rich and poor grows greater all the time as wages skyrocket at the top, while those at the bottom remain relatively unchanged. But a whole new set of people have come to the top. Now it is not only the party officials, the sycophants, the managerial class. It is the scientists, the technicians, the university professors who are elbowing their way in. These are the new *élite* who draw the big pay, with salaries ranging up to $1,500 a month for a rector of a university.

Not only are these salaries far in excess of their fellows' in their workers' state, but they are also a great deal higher than salaries their opposite numbers receive in our society. And while I listened to this young student tell me of his family holidays at Sochi and the yacht they sail on the Black Sea in the summertime, I could not help wondering if we in the West would be able to maintain our equality with the Soviet Union in the technical world of tomorrow, with our own low pay scales for this sort of person—and consequent shortage of them at the present time.

"Kazakhstan is the fastest-growing agricultural area in the Soviet Union." That is what Mohammed Galiyev, President of the Institute of Agriculture in Alma-Ata, told me. More and more people are coming to Central Asia from other parts of the Soviet Union.

"Why do they come?" I asked.

"Enthusiasm," he replied, "patriotism, and the desire to make the country big."

It is certainly a big country. A few years ago this was a desert waste, peopled only by a few nomad Kazakh cattle breeders. Today fifty million acres of virgin soil have been put under the plough.

Except for the Russian Republic, this is the biggest producer of grain in the Soviet Union—and it aims to be the biggest. All main crops are grown here, wheat, barley, rye, beets, corn, flax. Cattle breeding and sheep breeding have been developed; 12 per cent of the beef and 20 per cent of the wool in the Soviet Union come from Kazakhstan.

The chief problem in developing this area for agriculture is the minimal rainfall (average: 320 mm. per annum). Soviet scientists have tackled this problem with characteristic audacity. "If there isn't enough rain to grow wheat," they say, "we'll make a new kind of wheat we *can* grow!"

Of course, more orthodox scientists will say on this subject that, if you breed a grain that will grow without water, you breed an inferior strain that may be no use to anybody. Be that as it may, the opening of Central Asia to agriculture is one of the most daring feats of Soviet development and, if successful, could have incalculable effects on Soviet and world markets.

I obtained permission from President Galiyev to visit a few experimental stations on the plain outside Alma-Ata. Here, tests were under way at dozens of mobile laboratories, dotted over the countryside, to determine the best strains, soils and methods for raising crops in prevailing climatic conditions.

The outstanding agricultural scientist in this field is Mme N. L. Udolskaya, whom I met. Fiftyish, maternal, but rather a detached person, she was plainly dressed, with her hair tied in the typical Soviet bun. As an authority on plant genetics, she is quite famous, I was told. Her work has been mainly in the area of spring wheat. She published a book on the subject in Omsk in 1956, in which she showed how winter wheat may be converted into spring wheat, thus increasing the crop prospects.

I found Mme Udolskaya in the fields, working with her own variety of wheat, Kazanskay 126. This strain, she believes, is not only rust-resistant and smut-resistant, but also drought-resistant, although on the latter problem she was not prepared to say that a break-through had been achieved.

I noted that much of the scientific work in agriculture was being done by women in the Soviet Union. This, she said, is because plant breeding is a woman's work. "We are patient and men have too hard hands," she said. "Corn is like a child. It needs respect, good food and much attention."

I asked her why she, personally, had taken up this work.

"Because women in the Soviet Union must work alongside the men," she replied. "Our women are not like yours—living only to please their husbands. They have more important things to do."

A little taken aback, I murmured something to the effect that men in our country strive to please their wives and that most of the money in North America is spent by women anyway.

"Oh, money!" said Mme Udolskaya, with contempt. "We don't care about money any more. It is only work that matters!"

And that was that.

CHAPTER

10

UZBEKISTAN—AN ESSAY IN SOVIET COLONIALISM

Flight to Tashkent;
a luxury hotel with an unusual fly-trap;
façade and reality in Central Asia; an Uzbek mud town;
Russian imperialism; a policy of "beneficial conquest";
progress under Communism;
Uzbek art is not in the plan; whither Soviet Asia?

One hour's flying time to the south of Alma-Ata, along the foot-hills of the Himalayas, on the borders of Afghanistan, is another part of the patchwork of Soviet Central Asia—the "indepen-dent and autonomous" Soviet Socialist Republic of Uzbekistan.

The country below us as we flew was mountainous and bar-ren, with scarcely a sign of human habitation—a vast plateau of rock and sand, the fringe of the Kara Kum—the Black Desert. One could not help thinking of the countless caravans that came this way to carry riches to Europe from Cathay, to carry ad-venturers and merchants and pilgrims to their deaths in the terrible emptiness of the Hungry Steppe.

Then the scene changed. The land fell away into pleasant valleys, the green of a great oasis loomed into view, and the plane came down swiftly over a huge, sprawling city of tree-lined avenues; over gardens, orchards, and the glinting silvery-green of the rice fields.

We landed in Tashkent, capital of Uzbekistan.

The central hotel in Tashkent is a brand-new building in the Uzbek style—the only one I ever saw in Uzbekistan. The portico is supported by tall, fluted columns of white stone, extending from the ground floor to the flat roof. The interior of the portico is faced with blue glazed tiles, occasionally decorated with the emblems of the hammer and sickle and the dove.

Work on the building was still proceeding in the rear wings when I arrived, and the air was filled with dust and hammering. We were lodged in comfortable suites consisting of a private hallway, a large sitting-room equipped with television, and a bedroom with twin beds. There were the usual appurtenances, plus two large glass cabinets, filled with cut glass.

In spite of the newness and sumptuousness of the suite, I could not help noticing that the floor-boards were old and oily and some were actually loose. The bathroom plumbing also appeared to be salvage, and the toilet bowl leaked profusely over the cracked tiles of the floor.

As I was going down to dinner, a strange new smell greeted my nostrils. It permeated every corner of the building, and was to become so closely associated with my stay in Tashkent that I cannot recall the place yet without a faint accompaniment of nausea. I tracked down its source to the corridor leading from the main lobby to the dining-room.

This corridor was a long passage, connecting the main building with one of the wings. It was dimly lit by a few overhead bulbs and furnished with an assortment of bare wooden tables, each covered with saucers containing a white, glutinous substance that I ascertained to be sour milk. Thousands of flies were swarming over the milk, in which they were caught and killed.

The stench of this fly-trap was so great that it took my appetite entirely away, and I had to approach the dining-room on all future occasions by going outside and walking around the building to a side entrance. Even so, all the food was tainted with a flavour of sour milk, which reduced my diet throughout the stay to little else than freshly cut melons and champagne.

In the morning, we sallied forth to see the town. An Intourist limousine was put at our disposal, and also the services of an Uzbek interpreter—an agreeable young man who turned out to be not Uzbek, but Jewish. Aron Aronov was a creditable product of the Soviet university system. Smart, alert and dressed with a neatness that seems to elude his Russian comrades, Aron seemed to belong to our world. His thinking, however, was conditioned entirely by the requirements of a Marxist education. Everything, according to Aron, was for the best in the best of all possible worlds.

We spent the day looking at the monuments of Soviet progress: Red Square and the massive statue of Lenin in front of the red-granite Presidium of the Uzbek Republic, the Young Pioneers' Palace, the Opera and Ballet Theatre—all structures of formidable size.

There were also glimpses of the old Russian merchants' houses, with whitewashed walls and gabled roofs, along embankments that often rose six or eight feet above the level of the road—leafy promenades, arched over by pyramidal poplars, by lindens, massive oaks, and plane trees.

We stopped occasionally to inspect parks dedicated to the heroes of the Revolution. Although nicely laid out in a formalistic manner, they appeared unkempt, with grass a foot high in places and many rank weeds. The only gardening I saw done was by a pair of women on hands and knees, cutting the grass border with what seemed to be nail-scissors. Otherwise the parks were deserted.

The Grand Bazaar, on the other hand, teemed with humanity —a labyrinth of tin sheds and open stalls, where goods of every description were pawed over by a curious throng, half Russian, half Uzbek, the men mostly in European dress, the native women in *khalats,* loose gowns of striped cotton in white, black and yellow, which are characteristic Uzbek dress.

The purchasers were certainly more interesting than the purchases. Almost nothing of any value was to be found on any of these stalls; there were a few rugs dyed in garish colours, utterly unlike the world-famed Bokhara rugs of olden times; cheap watches, old bedsteads, broken, moth-eaten sofas. A welcome interlude was provided by the *shashlik* man, who is the Central Asian equivalent of the hot-dog man. On a raised brazier, rather like a mobile barbacue, he grilled his spears of spiced mutton and offered them for ten roubles ($1) apiece.

On Karl Marx Street, the main thoroughfare of the new town, I visited the biggest department store, the better to assess the purchasing value of the Uzbek rouble. Here all goods were new, displayed in little alcoves off the main floor. Downstairs, most of the products seemed to be tinware, crockery and other household effects, in very restricted quantities. A short length of rope fetched one dollar.

Up the uncarpeted wooden stairs, dry goods were on sale on the second floor. Men's suits of coarse quality and shapeless cut, with untapered legs and double-breasted coats, were fetching $160. The only attractive items were the small, square Uzbek skull-caps, nicely embroidered, for seven or eight dollars. Yet such was the excess of demand over supply that the crush was like bargain day in Eaton's basement.

"But where can I find an antique shop?" I enquired.

Aron, my guide, shrugged his shoulders impatiently. Brimful of facts and figures relating to Soviet progress, he was distinctly impatient of such anti-social pursuits as antique hunting.

"If you are looking for antiquities," he said, "I'm afraid you won't find any. The past belongs to the museums. History for us begins in 1917."

But history will not be silenced. It cannot be hidden behind the hastily erected façade, the Marx-Lenin Squares, the statues of Lenin, the heavy, ugly architecture that characterizes "Russian Modern". It speaks out from the very stones.

Setting out alone from the hotel at dusk, I walked in the direction of the river. The streets were filled with strollers at this hour. Most of the merchants' houses along the way appeared to be shared now by groups of families, eight or ten of whom were sitting outside each, taking the evening air.

I passed a long compound, protected by earthworks twenty feet high, topped by barbed wire and watch-towers. Searchlights played around the perimeter and uniformed guards patrolled the top of the embankment. Judging by the size and the precautions, I took this to be a very large place of detention indeed.

Soon I came to the river that separates the new town from the old. Crossing over an iron bridge, I followed the foot-path along the bank. On the way, I made a map of my route so I might retrace my steps, no printed map being available. I did not appear to be followed, and even the few fishermen beside the stream showed scant interest in me, and ignored my greeting.

A long, low mud wall extended along the river, about three hundred yards back from the bank. It had few openings and it was only by climbing the branch of a tree that I was able to see over it. On the other side I glimpsed, in the fast-failing light, a congeries of straw huts and hovels, as far as the eye could see. Here, I eventually estimated, most of the Uzbek people in this city of 700,000 live.

Spying a narrow entrance in the wall, I made for it. Down a dusty street, I encountered swarms of bare-foot children, but few adults, except for women filling their pitchers at the public hand pump. The traffic consisted mostly of native *arbas* or high-wheeled carts—often with inflated rubber tires—and an occasional Model-T Ford truck.

The buildings were entirely of mud, and the mud bricks of a brick-yard lay in ordered rows for drying. A few houses had second stories, with open screens of hemp and roofs of straw. Pushing open a door, I slipped inside. I found myself in a private compound, apparently shared by six or eight houses belonging to the same family or tribe.

Under a grape arbour, around an open fire, some women were rolling and baking their flat bread. They wore *khalats*, each of the identical, gaudy Uzbek pattern. The men-folk, in

European dress and skull-caps, sat cross-legged on brightly coloured rugs. Some played the mournful, twangling Uzbek music on the *rubob,* a stringed instrument. An air of utmost, hopeless poverty pervaded the scene.

This, of course, is nothing new to Asia. Squalor, misery and privation are the lot of human beings in all the lands of the East, from Cairo to Hong Kong. But at least Tashkent gives the lie to the Soviet propaganda that claims that the lot of man has been bettered for the greater number under Communism. The mass of the Uzbek people in Tashkent are evidently living today exactly as they lived for centuries before Communism came to Central Asia.

The Uzbeks are a people of proud and ancient lineage. Tough, resilient, resourceful, often merciless, they have warred upon one another and upon the world since the dawn of history.

Here arose the successive waves of conquest under Genghis and Tamerlane that beat upon the distant walls of Europe, until Rome and Paris trembled. Down the centuries, these Khanates and Emirates resisted all encroachments by the great imperial powers upon their independence. Merv, Khiva, Kokand, Bokhara, Samarkand—the names have always spelt mystery and intrigue. Few travellers from the outside world ever penetrated their fastnesses—fewer still ever left alive.

In the mid-1840's, newspapers and drawing-rooms in England were a-buzz with the story of two English soldiers, Colonel Stoddart and Captain Connelly, who called upon the Emir of Bokhara in an attempt to make a treaty with him on behalf of the British Government. For their pains, they were tossed in a vermin pit, where they were kept for two years until the flesh was largely eaten off their bodies. They were then publicly beheaded.

The Emir Nasrullah was said to be mad. But he was not too mad to frustrate all attempts to draw him into either of the great power blocs of his day—that of imperial Britain, and that of czarist Russia. A British expeditionary force was turned back at Kabul in neighbouring Afghanistan. The steadily advancing Russian forces were delayed and deceived into signing, in 1868, a treaty that guaranteed the independence of Bokhara until the fall of the empire.

But the days of independence were nearly over. In 1864 Turkestan fell to the Czar, and in 1865 the Imperial Army occupied Tashkent. In the scramble for Asia, the territories north of the Himalayas fell to Russia, while those to the south were spoils for the Western powers.

With the twentieth century, the ebb-tide of colonialism set in and the Western powers began their retreat. Britain left India, Holland abandoned Indonesia, France gave up Indo-China; but Russia remained in Central Asia—"welcomed," as the Soviet history books say, "by Uzbek leaders and people in the name of socialist unity and progress."

Far from condemning czarist imperial ambitions, the Soviets applaud them. "True," says the Soviet text-book, "this was a policy of conquest pursued by the czarist government, but the subsequent course of development showed that objectively it played a most beneficial role in the destinies of the peoples of the area." (*Socialist Culture of Uzbek People,* by T. N. Kari-Niazov, Moscow, 1958.)

The "beneficial role" was, of course, the opening up of Asia to Soviet development and control. This was not accomplished, however, without some difficulty and embarrassement. When the October Revolution occurred in Petrograd in 1917, it was echoed by an immediate outbreak of anti-Russian revolt in Central Asia.

The Soviets managed to secure the key city of Tashkent, and hoisted the hammer and sickle in place of the imperial eagle over the viceroy's palace. But their hold was precarious. In March, 1918, the Bolsheviks attacked Bokhara, and were soundly defeated by the Emir's army. On March 25th they signed a treaty with the Emir recognizing Bokhara as an independent state.

The Soviets now resorted to the tactics they have since made familiar the world over. Unable to gain their objective by direct assault, they employed the methods of infiltration that became their specialty. A Young Bokharan Communist Party was set up under the leadership of the son of one of the biggest capitalists in Bokhara, Faisullah Khojaev.

In the summer of 1920, the government of Bokhara was overthrown by an internal revolt, aided by the Red Army from Tashkent. The young Emir fled across the border to Afghanistan, taking as much of the national cash as he could carry. A revolutionary government was set up, headed by Faisullah Khojaev, who later became president of the newly created Soviet Republic of Uzbekistan. The colonization of Central Asia was complete.

It was interesting to stroll around the exhibits in the Museum of Uzbek History, a small and rather dilapidated building in Tashkent. Around the dark and dingy walls were displays in glass cases, and modelled scenes illustrating historic events in the life of Central Asia. Copious notes in Russian emphasized the revolutionary role of early Uzbek intellectuals, such as Abu Ali Ibn Sinna (980-1057), a doctor of medicine whose books were burned by the rulers of that day on religious grounds, and Ulugbeg, grandson of the Emperor Tamerlane, who made a catalogue of the stars and was burned alive for his pains.

My young guide, Aron, pointed up the moral of the tale. "The Soviet intelligentsia of Uzbekistan," he said, "is well aware that it is the Communist Party that has opened up our country to development."

There was a glass case in which were displayed the state robes of the last Emir—"a very bad man who was inordinately fond of children," Aron explained, and gave an account of the unorthodox arrangements in the Emir's harem, which was apparently inhabited equally by boys and by girls.

Having disposed, morally, of the Emir, Aron proceeded to deal with the nationalist opposition. Murals around the gallery depicted the terrorist activities of the *basmachis*, the native insurgents who waged war on the Soviets. These gross, wicked-looking men, in native *khalats* and turbans, were shown attacking peaceful villages, torturing progressive young Communists (in European dress), looting, and murdering the inhabitants.

"But the Soviet power soon triumphed," Aron assured me—omitting to mention that Faisullah Khojaev himself, the erstwhile President, was convicted in the spectacular trial of 1938 on his own confession of seeking to wreck the industry and agriculture of Uzbekistan, with the ultimate objective of converting it into a British colony!

Soviet policy in Uzbekistan has been ruthless, making Western colonial policy seem amateurish in comparison. Non-Communist Uzbeks were purged and executed. Uzbek dress was replaced with Russian dress in public. The Uzbek script, similar to Arabic, has been replaced with the Cyrillic script used by the Russians.

Furthermore, a flood of Russian settlers descended on Uzbekistan, swamping the indigenous population. Out of a total of eight million, five and a half million people are now Uzbek and the remainder Russian. The impression that emerges is that Uzbekistan is becoming more and more colonized by Russia.

I discussed this with a young Uzbek intellectual, Sharif Sherinbaev, Chairman of the Uzbek Society for Cultural Relations with Foreign Nations. He received me in one of the musty old offices, filled with czarist bric-a-brac, that so often serve for Soviet government departments.

A tired-looking man, with that somewhat strained, haughty manner that Communist officials adopt on meeting Westerners, he invited me to sit down in an arm-chair, while he took up position behind a formidable desk for what was evidently to be a well-prepared lecture.

"Here in the Uzbek Republic," he began, "we are all equal, both Uzbek and Russian. There is complete integration. Uzbek children and Russian children play together, go to the same nurseries and schools. Uzbeks eat and live beside Russians in the best hotels. There is equal opportunity for all." I did not say anything about the vast Uzbek mud town across the river.

He assured me that all high offices in the Government are held by Uzbeks—the Chairman of the Council of Ministers, the Secretary of the Communist Party; even the President is an Uzbek woman! But who makes the Seven-Year Plan? Who sets the examination papers in the schools? "We are grateful for Moscow's help in these matters," he replied.

Mr. Sherinbaev went on to list the benefits that Uzbekistan has to be grateful for. Before the Revolution the nation was illiterate; now there are more than 6,000 schools; there are 109 research institutes, 33 technical institutes, 2 universities, and 2 agricultural academies. Industry did not exist before the Revolution. Now there are chemical, mining, gas, and cotton industries, and 160,000 kilometres of canals for irrigation.

He really began to warm to his subject. Not only was Uzbekistan far advanced from what it was in feudal times, it was already ahead of the capitalist world. "We produce more cotton than Brazil, Turkey, Iran and other capitalist countries; our tractors and cotton-picking machines are better than American ones; we have already overtaken America in geology, physics, and chemistry."

I asked Mr. Sherinbaev if he would document Uzbekistan's world lead in geology. He referred to a book published by a professor in the Uzbek Academy of Sciences on methods of "geological forecasting", that is, determining the nature of deposits without digging. The book, he said, was acknowledged by American authorities as first in its field.

"So Uzbekistan has overtaken America with one book?"

"Not only with one book. Our professor has written three others since then!"

Well may America tremble!

Before I left, Mr. Sherinbaev told me something personal about himself. His father and his grandfather before him, he said, were slaves. His father was sold in the slave market at Bokhara for 180 roubles (today $18). "And that's why we hate capitalism!" he concluded vehemently.

This appalling simplification explains much of the Soviet success in Asia. By associating capitalism with their feudal past and by representing Communism as the sole possible liberating force, the Soviets have been able to enlist the support of a large proportion of the people.

Perhaps a useful yardstick in determining the extent of Russian colonialism in Soviet Central Asia would be to see the fate of Uzbek art. For this purpose, I called at the Uzbek Museum of Art in Tashkent. I was greeted by the custodian, a Russian lady, who had been warned of my arrival and kindly consented to conduct me herself.

I have found it advisable, in dealing with Soviet officialdom, not to beat about the bush. If you have an objective, you have to launch an offensive on all fronts at once to get to it. So I began by saying that I had come to study Uzbek art, I wanted to see Uzbek art and nothing else but Uzbek art.

The Russian lady bowed and led the way to a gallery of Russian paintings of the 19th century. After a suitable show of politeness, I returned to the attack. "Where is the Uzbek gallery?" I enquired.

In vain. For an hour and a half, I looked at painting, statuary, miniatures and furniture by Russian artists of the Czarist period. I am afraid my admiration fell some way short of the desired degree.

Then I grasped it—this *was* Uzbek art, as the Soviets conceive it. Uzbekistan is part of the Soviet Union, therefore all art, by artists of whatever race, is Uzbek art. I changed my request. Could I see art by artists of Uzbek, that is to say of Turki-Mongol, racial origin?

I was led to another gallery where a different lady, also Russian, awaited me. The room was carpeted with wine-red Bokhara rugs and contained some interesting exhibits of traditional Uzbek arts—mosaics, pottery, and hand-painted furniture, which I was told were new.

I had found such objects to be virtually unobtainable in

Tashkent. Merchants had told me that new Bokhara rugs of traditional style and quality were unknown. I had been unable to locate any pottery, and I had bought one small hand-painted box, measuring five inches by eight inches, for $28 in an "art store" on Karl Marx Street.

Consequently, I enquired if it was possible to see any of the craft workshops myself. The custodian of the collection gave me an address, which I followed up immediately. The head office was located downtown and the assistant manager, another Russian lady, received me. She readily agreed to my request, and an appointment was made to show me the wood-painting shop that afternoon.

But after this, things took a peculiar turn. I ordered the car for two o'clock, but it did not come. By four o'clock I had become impatient and demanded another car from the Intourist office. Then I was advised to abandon my project. I insisted. Wasn't it enough that the manager had agreed to my visit?

Tamara, my interpreter, intervened. "No," she said, "you should know that our citizens cannot agree to anything like that without higher authority."

I protested that in Canada a citizen needed no Government permission in order to show his shop or factory to a foreigner.

Tamara shrugged. "Then you haven't got the right system," she remarked dryly.

I never found the reason. But evidently Uzbek art is not in the Plan.

There is no doubt that the Soviets have brought progress to Central Asia—a dull, shabby kind of progress, but progress all the same. But is this the ultimate goal for a great and ancient civilization—to be relegated to the museums and to be replaced by a Russianized way of life, with Russian dress, Russian architecture, Russian writing, Russian education, Russian art, and above all, more and more Russian people?

CHAPTER

11

GLIMPSES OF THE NEW ASIA

A visit to the Central Asian University;
the culture binge; an open-air play; the Soviet version of history;
a cotton factory helps fulfil the Seven-Year Plan;
the Grand Mosque at Tashkent at the hour of prayer;
what is the meaning of "holy"?

"The greatest thing that Soviet power has done in Uzbekistan is to make education available to all." Aron, my Tashkent guide, was talking. "In old times, only the rich were educated; now we are 100 per cent literate. In old times we had to bow low before the Emir; now we are all equal. I can slap the Chairman of the Council of Minsters on the back. Isn't this better?"

Such is the logic of the new Asia. Because feudalism was overthrown by Communism, this is the only way it could have happened. Because the people have been raised out of slavery and into Communism, this is the only way to live.

At the University of Central Asia, in Tashkent, I saw in action the process of educating for Communism. A musty old yellow-brick building of czarist times (apart from a few show places, it is remarkable how much of the day-to-day life of the country is carried on in these decaying survivals), the university accommodates four thousand students.

They come from thirteen different nations, not only from Central Asia but from China, Korea, Viet Nam, Indonesia.

They stand around on the dusty street outside the university building—there appears to be no campus—solemn and unsmiling, clutching their heavy text-books of Marxism-Leninism. One wonders at such youthful gravity in the land where oppression has been abolished and the oppressed set free.

But it is a grim and serious world, the world of Marxist knowledge, filled with dialectical terrors: counter-revolutionary bourgeois nationalism, economic revisionism, foreign interventionism, Trotskyist blocs, and all the other terminology of the Soviet text-books. No wonder young minds quail at the dangers before them. Fortunately, say the text-books, "the October Revolution abolished the rule of the exploiters, it united the working masses and eliminated national oppression." So perhaps they may learn to smile, one day, after all.

It is not hard to see what drives these young people on. It is poverty. Only through education can they hope to escape from those single rooms, filled with the clamour of an entire family, lit by a single insufficient light-bulb in the ceiling, with no place to put one's books except the window-sill.

Education provides the single avenue to a better life—to a private room in a university residence at State expense, to the prospect of a job in the service of the State with the privilege of owning a private flat, a car, perhaps a *dacha* in the country. For this, it is worth getting up to attend classes at seven in the morning, slaving over home-work until late at night, and spending 10 per cent of the time on political studies, learning to give the correct answers on Marxism-Leninism, without which one cannot hope to graduate.

And behind this the greater question arises—whether the State, realizing the value of poverty as a spur to achievement, deliberately keeps the standard of living low, in order to assure a constant flow of serious, hard-working students, eager to put their services at its disposal. Such are the incentives of a have-not society.

A pleasant, youngish man, Rector Beliaff, received me in his office, a sunny room with Victorian furniture in dust-covers.

The University of Central Asia, he told me, was established by Lenin, who emphasized the importance of learning. "Without that," said the master, "there can be no politics; without that there are only rumours, gossip, fables and prejudice, but not politics."

Faculties included, besides Marxism-Leninism, physics, mathematics, history, philology, agriculture, and medicine. I asked how the quotas were set governing the number of students admitted to these faculties, and was told that this was controlled by Central Gosplan (the State Planning Commission)—thereby ensuring the exact number of scientists and technicians for State requirements.

I was also introduced to Mr. Abdul Rahman Hamarieff, the Professor of History. Born about 1900, he was, he said, illiterate before the revolution. In 1923, he graduated from university and became a village teacher. Now he has a son who is chief of the Department of Law in Tashkent and another who is a film producer in Moscow, a daughter who is a doctor of medicine, and one who is a medical student. So he is naturally convinced of the benefits conferred through Soviet education! I was told that in 1956 Uzbekistan held its first Congress of Intellectuals, attended by delegates representing the "125,000-strong Soviet intelligentsia of Uzbekistan". I did not, I'm afraid, find out how this "egg-head" census was actually taken.

Reverting to the subject of culture, I asked Mr. Hamarieff if Uzbek culture was being absorbed by Russian culture. He replied that this was impossible, since all culture in the Soviet Union has one socialist content and varies only in outward form.

"The main principle of cultural development is socialism," he said. "That is why eventually all cultures must have the same content under socialism."

The entire Soviet world of today is on a culture binge. Even in their moments of relaxation, the citizens of the new Asia are busy getting cultured. In the large public park in Tashkent there are numerous pavilions, cinemas, open-air theatres, band shells, and the like. They are laid out prettily, with well-lighted paths, ice-cream parlours, tea-houses along the way.

Some avenues are dedicated to the arts, with rows of poster-pictures in crude colours, representing the cultural pantheon—Gogol, Chekhov, Gorki, Maiakovsky, and Navoi (fifteenth century Uzbek poet), each mounted in a gimcrack frame and surrounded by a halo of bare light bulbs.

It is not always easy to find ordinary people, or even English-speaking students, who know what these great names represent —what Chekhov wrote, for instance. But everyone seems to accept the idea that it was these culture-heroes who "built Communism". I was all the more interested, therefore, to fall into conversation over a cup of tea with the director of the Tajik State Theatre, then performing in the open-air theatre. The bill was a Russian translation of the verse-drama *Maria Stuart* by the eighteenth-century German playwright, Schiller.

I expressed some astonishment at the ambitious choice of theatrical fare, and asked, perhaps a trifle anxiously, after the box-office. I was told they had played to packed houses, sold out weeks in advance. To what did he attribute this unaccountable passion for the German bard in Uzbekistan? The director replied: "All levels of our society are now equally cultured." I said this suggested a higher degree of culture in Uzbekistan than in America, where this play has probably not been presented for fifty years. "Why," he asked, somewhat patronizingly, "is the level of American culture so low?"

I replied that, whereas in the Soviet Union culture is obligatory, people in America choose their own entertainment. Hence only a small minority supports the serious theatre of its own free choice. He thought this over and then replied with satisfaction: "That shows your policy is a very bad one."

I decided to accept the director's kind invitation to see a performance of *Maria Stuart,* and presented myself at the gates shortly after the curtain had gone up. It was a pleasant theatre, enclosed by a high wall, open to the sky. The stage was large and well equipped, with provision for all possible scenic effects. Settings and costumes were equally sumptuous, and the whole production was on a scale far beyond the usual standard for an open-air show.

I was shown to a seat that had been kept for me in the second row, and found myself beside a middle-aged man who spoke a little English. He turned out to be a teacher of history in a secondary school, and we chatted about a variety of subjects during the interval. It was a relief to me to discover that the play bored him as much as it did me. (The reception by the audience was, in fact, so cool that I wondered if they had all fallen asleep.)

On the way home our paths lay together, and we discussed general topics while walking. I asked what he taught his pupils about the history of the Second World War. "I explain that the Soviet people defeated the fascists single-handed, after the Western Powers failed to intervene in time."

Having been in action with the Canadian forces in Europe for two years, I gave him an argument on this point. He was immovable. "Britain and America only intervened at the last moment, when it became plain that Germany was going to lose the war."

This argument was part of a larger thesis that he imparted to his students, in which Britain and America were the consistent enemies of peace-loving peoples all over the world. "In 1919, they invaded Russia on behalf of the White counter-revolutionaries; they intervened in Korea against the will of the people; they are oppressing working people today in countless countries such as South Vietnam, Nyasaland, and South America."

Somehow I had managed never to raise the ghost of Hungary in any of my conversations with Soviet people. This time I did. The history teacher was unimpressed. "It is well known that the anti-popular revolt in Hungary was the work of fascist reactionaries and foreign interventionists in the pay of American capitalists."

128

Nevertheless, I persisted, Hungary is not free. "You make a fetish of freedom in the West," he said. "Is it so important? We are giving Hungary good government. We are pouring in money. We are developing the economy. What does freedom matter?"

And what does the history professor teach his students about the intentions of America today? "I say they are surrounding us with bases. Is this not so? And what are bases for, except to attack the Soviet Union?"

"Do you really believe that?" I asked.

"Of course. That is what all working people in the Soviet Union believe."

I doubted his ability to speak for all the working people in the Soviet Union. I had talked to too many others who thought otherwise. But they were not paid to teach the official party line. A good question is: why does the party want this message taught in the schools? Does it really believe the message itself? Or is it part of a plan to subvert history?

Questions a Tashkent school-teacher could not answer for me.

Uzbekistan is the main cotton-growing area in the Soviet Union, a fact that probably explains why cotton balls form part of the State emblem and why the huge 57,000-seat stadium for sports (and political rallies) is called "the Cotton-Picking Stadium". The Stalin Cotton Mill, said to be the largest in the world, is also located in Tashkent.

Outside the factory gates stands a gigantic portrait of Stalin, which suggests that the process of de-Stalinization has not penetrated as far as Uzbekistan. In addition, there is a wall covered with photographs in gold frames—not, as I thought at first, war heroes who had given their lives for the motherland, but workers who had overfulfilled their quotas.

Other signs of State propaganda crowd the view. Posters along the walks of the workers' park, banners hanging from the ceiling of the workshop, all proclaim the objective of overtaking America, and urge workers to "Help fulfill the Seven-Year Plan", "Raise productivity by 8%", and "Observe the rules of Socialist duty".

I was conducted over the plant by the lady engineer in charge, Mrs. Tolstich, a sturdy, middle-aged woman with a big-boned face and deep-sunk, tired eyes. She wore a nondescript print dress and no jewellery or make-up.

Mrs. Tolstich bosses 17,000 workers, including her own husband. I asked if this situation led to any complications in her home life, but she assured me that she and her husband were on the best of terms. This factory, she told me, produces twenty tons of cotton a day. Combing and carding are done by automation, and the machines (bearing Leningrad trade-marks) seemed well worn but efficient. I heard that 70 per cent of the engineering staff were women.

Mrs. Tolstich began in this plant as a weaver; she went to night-school, and graduated as an engineer. Her studies comprised weaving, metal technology, political economy and Marxism-Leninism. I asked what use Marxism-Leninism was in her practical work. She said it was useful because she was in charge of training workers, and was able to give them leadership in "right thinking".

It is hard to discover the purpose behind this drive for production. It is true that consumer goods are desperately short in the Soviet Union. Finished cotton fabrics are limited to a few gaudy patterns. But relief of consumer scarcity is not one of the objectives of the Seven-Year Plan, which is almost wholly geared to an assault on Western economies.

Uzbekistan, I was told, means to overtake the USA in cotton production. It is noteworthy that the goal of an 8 per cent increase in cotton is exactly the same as the target in basic industry. Soviet cotton goods may soon flood the free markets of Asia, alongside Soviet steel, atomic plants, petroleum refineries, and Marxist-Leninist "right thinking".

An interesting area of impact between Soviet Communism and native Asian culture is in religion. By tradition, the peoples of Central Asia are Sunni Moslems of an ardent and fanatical faith. It was this faith, in part, that led them to wage a *jihad,* or holy war, on unbelievers in the fourteenth century that carried the Crescent into the heart of Europe. The Moslems of Central Asia were noted for their intolerance of any science or theology other than that revealed by the Prophet. Abu Ali ibn Sinna, the eleventh-century founder of Uzbek medicine, was exiled and his books burned as irreligious. The great Ulugbeg, grandson of Tamerlane, who made a catalogue of two thousand stars in the fifteenth century, was burned alive and his observatory destroyed. "There is no God but God."

How have the followers of Mohammed fared under the atheistic Soviet State? To find out, I paid a visit to the Great Mosque in Tashkent. It was noon on a Friday, the holy day at the hour of prayer. The sun was mercilessly hot and I was grateful for the shade of the big tree in the courtyard. The buildings of the Mosque and the *madrasseh,* or school of religion, were charming and stately with their white walls, domes and pointed Arabic arches, after the antique squalor and drab modernity of Tashkent.

At first the place seemed deserted, until I noticed row upon row of shoes, ranged by the hundreds on the steps of the mosque. The wearers were at prayer within. Afterwards they streamed out in bare feet, slipped into their shoes and shuffled off, proud and reserved but unafraid to be observed.

Then I met the Venerable Mufti, Zia Ud Din Eshon Babahan, who has jurisdiction over thirteen million Moslems in Soviet Central Asia. He was not, in actual fact, so very venerable, being a youngish man in his thirties, son of the last Mufti, who died in 1957 at the age of ninety-six. But he looked very colourful and distinguished in his high white turban and brightly coloured robes.

The Mufti showed me over the Mosque and the *madrasseh,* which is 370 years old. The school consists of a row of small rooms or cells, opening off a cloister in the courtyard. In these rooms the imams, or teachers, hold classes and expound the teachings of the Koran.

I asked how many imams were in training, but there was some hesitation on the part of the Mufti to reply, through my official interpreter, so I did not press the point. Instead, I asked if the number of believers was increasing. "Not less and not more than before," was the guarded reply. It seemed evident that his position was delicate and he was required to give only certain replies.

The State, he assured me, has nothing to do with the Church, although apparently the Church can do nothing without the State. Thus, the pilgrimage to Mecca, the "Glorious Haj", which every Moslem hopes to make before his death, can be undertaken only with State approval. While in the past many thousand pilgrims went to Mecca every year from Central Asia, this approval is now given to only twenty or twenty-five persons a year—that is, the capacity of one plane. The reason for this restriction, the Mufti was careful to point out, was the difficulty in obtaining visas for Soviet pilgrims in transit overland through non-socialist countries. No mention was made of any difficulty in obtaining exit visas from the Soviet Union.

We repaired to a banquet hall, where an Oriental feast was spread in overwhelming profusion. But first, we stopped beside a servitor who held a basin filled with water. I was invited to dip in my hands and the Mufti, in a traditional ceremony of hospitality, then dried them for me with a clean towel.

The table was spread with all manner of fruit, chicken, meat, flat unleavened bread, and bowls of a most delicious soup called *kovoorma*. The ingredients for the latter appeared to be fried mutton, potato, tomato, pepper, onion, salt and water. But the flavour must be a secret of the faithful alone!

Throughout the meal, which lasted all of two hours, we discussed points of faith. I enquired if it were possible to be a good Moslem and a Communist at the same time. The Mufti had probably handled this one before, because he replied with great dialectical aplomb. "A good Moslem," he said, "is one who has God in his heart. A good Communist is one who believes in the good of his country. Therefore it is possible to be both at one and the same time."

This answer, however, did not succeed in pleasing Aron. The interpreter pointed out that no one who believes in God can be a member of the Communist Party. A young man of the new school, he also bogged down on several of the theological terms used in our discussion. For example, I made use of the word "holy".

"What's that—holy?" he enquired.

I tried to explain.

"Oh, I see. You mean if you are a success at religion you're holy?"

I countered that being holy was rather a condition than an achievement. "It means being in a state of grace," I concluded.

"What's that—grace?" he asked.

"It's no use, you had better give it up," I advised him. "The words have passed out of your language."

12

SAMARKAND: JOURNEY'S END

A modern caravan on the Silk Road;
how to make shashlik;
the legend of Tamerlane, his conquests, his loves, his death;
Samarkand today; last glimpse of Tamara;
the park, the dance pavilion, and the Shah Zinda tombs;
beauty is not in the plan

We are the Pilgrims, master; we shall go
Always a little further.

The Silk Road ran for two thousand miles from Damascus, the
jewel of the Moslem Umayyad Empire, to Samarkand, one-
time Capital of the Earth, gleaming mysteriously blue on the
white desert of Central Asia. Along it, six hundred years ago,
travelled the caravans that carried the gorgeous and exotic traffic of the East: the silks, of course, the carpets, the ivory, the
frankincense and myrrh, the oil and spice, the rubies, jade, and
oriental pearls.

It was a grim and terrible journey. By day, there was the endless swaying of the camels and the litters that carried the mer-
chandise; but most of the travellers went on foot, over quick-
sands, salt marshes and treacherous mud flats. By night, there
was the filth and stench of the caravanserais, the mud huts
of the Turkomen, the smoke-filled tents of the Tatars, infested
with vermin and lice. At all times, there was the danger of raid-

ing bands, the parching sun, and the dust storms that concealed the way. And yet there was still a mystery that drew men on:

For lust of knowing what should not be known
We make the Golden Journey to Samarkand.

Fortunately the journey today is not so hazardous. Driving in a Soviet Zim limousine—something like a 1940 Cadillac—over the broiling Kara Kum Desert (120 degrees in the shade and no shade), I saluted the memory of those legendary caravans. We followed the foothills of the Tien Shan range in the valley of the Zaravshan, a strong-flowing river that gets nowhere. It sets out bravely across the desert but, like the lives and dreams of countless pilgrims, it is sucked into the hungry sand and vanishes.

In the heat of the day, we sought the shelter of the sparse trees that clustered around a wayside pool. The water was clear and deliciously cold, however—just right for a most refreshing swim. Our guide for this portion was Marius, a well-educated and intelligent Samarkand boy, who knew the roads and customs of the country. He demonstrated his skill at making *shashlik,* the favourite dish of Central Asia.

Marius began by soaking the ground well with water. He placed two stones about a foot apart and lit a small brush fire between them. Once it was crackling merrily, he sprinkled the blaze lightly with charcoal. Next came the preparation of the meat. Shashlik is made of mutton, cut in small lumps, big enough to skewer on a slender spear. The pieces of meat are interspersed with a small piece of fat, onion, garlic or other seasoning. The spears were then laid across the fire, suspended on the stones.

The result was the tastiest dish imaginable—but no doubt it needs to be cooked by a cheerful Uzbek boy and washed down with clear water from a desert pool on the road to Samarkand to be enjoyed to the fullest extent.

The Oasis of Samarkand stretches for many miles along the Zaravshan Valley, but the clusters of mud walls and straw roofs along the way gave small indication of the fabled glories of this legendary city. Then, from a small rise of ground, I glimpsed it —shimmering blue on the horizon, as the sun glinted from the blue tile of its domes and minarets, all veiled in a golden haze of heat and blowing sand.

How extraordinary it seemed that this city should have been built on the arid roof of the world, thousands of miles from the haunts of civilized men—"a blue jewel on a withered hand"! That it should have been a magnet for the imagination down the centuries, as one of the wonders of the world, is perhaps the greatest mystery of all.

Of course, we know how it came about. In the fourteenth century a certain keeper of wild horses, living on the steppes of Central Asia, set out to conquer the world. His name was Tamerlane. The world he knew was a bleak horizon filled with desert and mud-walled Tatar villages. At the head of a small band of horsemen, he succeeded in making himself a local khan.

But then other horizons hove into view; from the east, the Mongol Empire sent its Golden Horde against him. He defeated them. To the north lay the Land of Shadows, the abode of the Princes of Muscovy. He sacked Moscow, reduced Kiev to a tributary, and carried fire and sword into Poland and Lithuania. New horizons opened to the south in the Land of the Sun; he reduced Turkey to ashes and carried the Sultan Bayzid around with him in a cage, he siezed the treasury of Ind and slew a hundred thousand at Delhi, he razed Baghdad to the ground and built a hundred and twenty pyramids of the skulls of its inhabitants. Tamerlane, the Emperor of the Tatars, died feared with a morbid terror by nearly all mankind.

Yet he built a city that was in its day the most beautiful in the world. After he had conquered the earth (all, that is, except a few unimportant principalities of Europe and the forbidden reaches of Cathay), he brought back with him architects, craftsmen and artisans who were ordered to build a capital finer than any he had destroyed. And so, in his lifetime, there came into being that wonder of the desert, Samarkand.

He built it blue, because blue was the favourite colour of the Tatars—the colour of the endless sky on their horizon. Over the archways, the domes and minarets of the new city, a blue glaze was spread, laced with gold and silver lettering. It was a massive city. Twice Tamerlane ordered the work torn down and built again—larger.

Gardens were everywhere and dripping fountains. Within, the pavilions and palaces were a mass of flowers—but all the flowers were mosaics. In the courtyards stood trees with trunks of gold, branches of silver and fruit of precious stones. When the Emperor went forth, slaves tossed gold dust into the air and pearl seeds under the hooves of his horse.

Tamerlane's last wish was to build for himself a fitting tomb. He searched the world for a design. And then he saw it: the immense towering dome of the great Umayyad mosque at Damascus. He ordered his architects to copy the design; and then he burned the mosque, with all of Damascus, to the ground—in order to rebuild it in Samarkand nearer to the heart's desire.

Tamerlane died in 1405, two years before the Gur Emir Mausoleum was finished. When he was buried, he caused to be inscribed on his tomb a terrible curse upon the world if ever it should be opened. It was opened, however, by a professor of the Soviet Academy of Sciences, who no doubt had a healthy Soviet contempt for superstition.

Professor Gerasimov sought proof for the legend that Tamerlane was lame. (The English version of his true name, which was Timur, is itself a corruption of Timur-the-lame.) The opening took place on June 21st, 1941. The next day, as all the world knows, Hitler invaded Russia! And Timur *was* lame.

I stood a long time in the white, sun-drenched courtyard of the Gur Emir, turning these things over in my mind. I had descended the narrow stairway that leads to the dark cavern of the tomb and gazed upon the small black rock (nevertheless said to be the largest piece of nephrite in the world), that marks the grave of him who declared himself the "scourge of God and Lord of All the Earth". I had come up again into the bright Central Asian day. Somehow, Tamerlane the man and his pain-wracked body, his compulsive ambition, his pyramids of skulls, seemed unutterably far away. Only the blue-tiled mausoleum had survived, joyous and perfect as on the day it was built. Somewhere in this was the answer.

The central square of Tamerlane's city, called the Registan, stands today in form and aspect as it stood when it arose six hundred years ago. The Registan had a grace of proportion that earned it the commendation of an earlier traveller, Lord Curzon, as "the noblest square in the world".

Open on one side to the street, it is faced on the other sides by three *madrassehs*, or Moslem colleges: the Golden Mosque *madrasseh*, a-shimmer with turquoise tile; the *madrasseh* of Ulugbeg, built by Tamerlane's grandson, who spent his time charting the heavens while evil men stole away his earthly domains; and the Shir Dar, which means Lion Bearing and carries a great golden lion over its central arch.

The whole picture is framed by four blue minarets, incredibly slender and tall, one leaning perilously as a result of the many earthquakes in this region. A few frayed ropes hold up the tottering giant, but surely it will take only a tremor, a puff of wind to bring it crashing to the ground and shatter the illusion forever.

Little is being done to repair the ravages of time and nature. Grass grows between the cobble-stones of the square and from the cracks in the blue domes; the tile falls off the walls in avalanches and lies where it falls. I saw some heaps of fourteenth-century tile shovelled out to form a roadbed for passing trucks.

But for the moment it is there, as it was in the Golden Age, when Tamerlane reviewed his army, when the ambassadors of foreign powers came to plead for their nations to be spared, or when the Emperor brought home the kings and queens of the earth captive and in chains.

I heard a number of pretty stories in Samarkand. For example, there is the story of Tamerlane's favourite wife, a Chinese princess named Khanum Bibi—naturally we came to call her "Honey Baby". It seemed that when Tamerlane set out to conquer the world, he left behind a young Persian architect with orders to build Honey Baby a beautiful palace. And, of course, as young people will, they fell in love.

At first Honey Baby tried to dissuade him. She offered him any of the forty maidens who waited upon her. And to illustrate her point she put before him a little demonstration. The young architect was presented with a tray full of forty coloured eggs, each different. Said the princess: like women, they seem different on the outside, but on breaking them open each is found to be the same on the inside.

Her lover was not impressed. In a demonstration of his own, he offered the lady a tray with two glasses, each containing a clear liquid. One was water and the other was vodka. Which proved, he said, that although women may seem to be alike, one is as water and the other is as fire! Honey Baby gave in.

The palace of Honey Baby still stands today, a gigantic ruin, its cupola pierced in half, it is said, by a Russian shell during the campaign of 1868. Not far away is the enclosed avenue of tombs where the little princess lies buried, along with other favourites of the Emperor.

It is a long stairway, flanked on either side by richly decorated mausoleums, leading upward, as it seems, to some earthly paradise. Shah Zinda, it is called—the Living King. A peaceful and fitting end to the passions and turmoil of Samarkand's Golden Age.

The streets of modern Samarkand present a varied and interesting picture—typically Russian in layout, overwhelmingly Asian in character. It is noteworthy that the Russians have been here since 1868, when the Imperial Armies wrested Samarkand from the Emir and established a forward base of operations in the town.

Hence the rows of whitewashed shops, single-storied, with small windows and wooden shutters, dating back to these times. Here and there, the modern Soviet cars negotiate the narrow streets. Russian traffic policemen direct the traffic from their standard pedestals in the centre of the road.

But all the rest is pure fairy tale. Like characters out of the *Thousand and One Nights* come the obese old men riding on tiny donkeys, mothers suckling children at the breast, swarthy men sitting cross-legged on a pile of rugs in a *chai khana* (tea house) drinking tea out of shallow cups, women in heavy black horse-hair veils, one-eyed beggars, mountebanks performing conjuring tricks—only the Just Caliph and the beautiful Scheherazade are missing.

Shopping with Marius, my guide, I learned that the pleasure of Oriental bargaining has gone too. Now no more can merchant and shopper enact their age-old ritual, accompanied with waving hands and appeals to Allah, in order to arrive at a price usually pre-ordained in the merchant's favour. Today the State sets all the prices, keeps all the profits.

Of the ancient ceramic art, I was able to discover only one example in a humble potter's shop on the Tashkent Road. I selected a plate of good design but inferior workmanship, with very thin glaze. Most of the pieces in the shop were badly flawed. I commented on the decline in craftsmanship to Marius.

"Well, what can you expect?" he asked loftily. "We don't need things like this any more. We can get *good* plates from Moscow now—and maybe from the United States one day!"

The hotel in Samarkand is an old-fashioned, two-story building of the czarist period, its interior hung with velvet drapes and the usual pictures of Lenin addressing the sailors at Petrograd, fraternizing with the students, and so on. My room opened on a balcony overlooking a courtyard. Here toward evening a hundred or more beds were set up in the open, to accommodate guests under the stars.

It was pleasant to sit out in the darkness, watching the stir and commotion as guests came and went, unrolling their turbans, drinking tea and bedding down, as candles were lit and conversation rolled on incomprehensibly. The only distraction was the loud-speaker plague, which filled the courtyard with a ceaseless medley of Oriental and European music, mixed with "news" and messages of exhortation and encouragement.

There is something intimidating about this constant public noise, with literally no refuge from sun-up until long after sundown from the voice of Big Brother. Little privacy remains in the world, even the privacy of our own thoughts, since the advent of the electronic age. But, at least, in other lands one can complain to the management if a neighbour's radio is too loud. What can one do in the Soviet Union, where the management *is* Big Brother?

We were nearing the end of our journey and this seemed the occasion for a little celebration. At dinner, we ordered a small banquet with the surplus Intourist coupons that remained. Tamara came down to the dining-room wearing her best red dress, red open-toed Indian sandals—the gift of an Indian tourist—and a string of Poppit pearls left with her by an American lady.

I had never seen her look so happy. I never got to know Tamara well. She acquitted herself efficiently throughout our tour, expressing at all times the correct attitudes demanded by her position, and palliating the crudity of the propaganda with an understanding of Western sensibilities rare in Soviet officials. But she had never revealed anything of herself to me.

For some reason, Samarkand answered a deep-seated need in her nature. "I love this place," she said over and over. I realized that this exotic flowering of an antique civilization was the one bright spot of colour in an otherwise singularly drab life.

The spell was broken, however, when the Russian lady in charge of the Intourist desk in the hotel came up to our table. Shaking her finger, she exchanged a few sharp words with Tamara.

"Ah, Tamara!" she exclaimed. "You look like an American woman now—you are not a good Russian woman any longer!"

This colloquy took place in Russian, which Tamara afterwards somewhat ruefully translated. The matter was dismissed with a laugh. But I could not help noticing that she removed the pearls from her neck at once.

In the evening there is little to do in Samarkand, except walk. Everybody walks, and most usually find their way to the park. People are encouraged to live in public, so that they are to be seen at all hours, strolling about in great herds, going home only to sleep. Part of the philosophy of "togetherness"—and, of course, it makes the task of supervision and indoctrination easier.

Among the attractions in the park was a sort of sawdust ring, surrounded by benches for spectators. Inside the ring, a hard-working State employee was busy organizing games. Many were childish games, like a version of musical chairs, but grown men joined in with gusto. Another game was a tug-of-war in which three participated on a circular rope.

An interesting thing about these games was that they called for group participation—never two competitors or teams. Further training for collectivism. I also noted that although both Uzbeks and Russians took part, the Uzbeks were Russianized in dress and manner. None of the old-style Uzbeks were in the park at all. Nevertheless, when one of these games broke up, I was followed by a group of Uzbek boys who wanted to confide in me. "Amerikanski very good," they said, doubtless mistaking my nationality, "*Ruski nyet!*"

The dance pavilion provided one of the most incongruous sights in this city of legend and romance: an open enclosure, large enough to accommodate several hundred persons; admission one rouble—ten cents. Inside, they whirled around to polkas, tangos and fox-trots, played over the loud-speaker—men in shapeless, baggy trousers and cloth caps, women with frizzy hair and sack-like dresses; the men dancing with the men, and the women with the women—all somehow completely sexless.

The more I have looked about in the Soviet Union, the more it is apparent that this country has achieved just what it claims —the dictatorship of the proletariat. The entire nation, of many races and cultures, has been standardized on the norm of the Russian factory worker. In this expressionless mass, hardly an individuality stands out, a quick laugh or a sensitive face. It is a terribly barren world, so barren that when one thinks of the infinite variety of people, opinions, dress, tastes, pursuits and pleasures in the world outside, the Soviet world seems like one great prison.

Some of the inmates know their plight, of course, which is essentially a bondage of the spirit rather than the flesh. For them, their lot must be terribly hard. Most, however, seem passively content. The possibilities of life are kept sedulously from them. It may take decades for them to discover these possibilities for themselves. Meanwhile, they doggedly pursue the goal that has been set them—to overtake America. And they may, indeed, do this, in terms of producing steel, turbine generators, atomic power stations, and *sputniks*. But they do not yet guess what America—or, in fact, life—really is.

It was late at night. The dance pavilion was closed and the gates of the park locked; the streets were deserted. But I could not return to bed. Next morning I was to leave Samarkand and begin the long journey home, half-way across the earth.

Through the dim-lit streets I made my way across the town to the hillside, where the domes of the Shah Zinda tombs shone white in the dying light of the moon. The world of men was silent and dark. It was the ghosts who were alive now.

I sat upon a broken wall. At my feet lay small pieces of tile, in a heap of rubbish. I picked one up. It was only a bit of sunbaked clay, but on its surface were traced a flower and a leaf of most exquisite design, colour and beauty.

That was it—beauty, a word seldom used in the Soviet world. Whatever else is to be found here—science, industry, education —there is little that is beautiful. Beauty is not in the Plan. But some day it will flower again here, as it did long ago, and will transform the barren world and the lives of men and give them meaning.

AFTERWORD

A contradictory world;
Russia is just beginning; the Seven-Year Plan—can they do it?
Soviet military and economic strategy; what do we want to do?
challenge and response in education; and in the under-
developed areas;
toward a redirection of material and spiritual values

This has been a glimpse of a most contradictory world. Every-one who visits it sees it differently. This is not only because of the multiplicity of viewpoints; it is also because its Soviet masters choose to create confusion by revealing different aspects to different people. It may be thought, for instance, that I have concentrated on the dark aspects of the Soviet scene, to the exclusion of its "uplifting" side.

Some may ask me: why did you not visit developments such as Dubno, the great nuclear-research institute with the largest atom-smasher in the world, or Novosibirsk, the "science city"; or interview "positive" personalities, such as Mme Furtseva, the leading woman parliamentarian, or Professor Alexander Nesmeyanov, the director of the Soviet space probe, and many others? The answer is that indeed I wished and pleaded and fought to do so, but this was denied to me. I do not know why.

Instead of the monolithic State, however, I saw the multi-faceted human picture, which is composed of an infinity of aspects, many or most of which are unrelated to political theory or doctrine. I met people, some Communist but many not; I saw them in their work and at home and in their private lives, and I learned from their own mouths how many of them think and feel. This, I believe, is even more indicative than *sputniks* or party propaganda of whither the Soviet society is tending and what is going on in the human substratum on which it rests.

It is a *changing* world. The Soviet citizen still lives under a gigantic tyranny, if only in the sense that the State orders his existence from the birth to the grave. Yet many of the people we met told us that they were never so free in their lives. Of course, they are not free, as we conceive of freedom. They cannot travel to the West, as we go to the Soviet Union. They cannot even travel from one place to another inside their own country without a visa. They cannot read what they wish, but only what their Government chooses to give them. They cannot strike for higher wages, because their trade unions are Government-controlled. But they can and do speak out against these things now. This in itself is a great advance.

Then again, the Soviet people are very poor, living close to the border-line of subsistence. Yet the ordinary people, who took us into their homes and spread their bread and cucumbers and salt before us, said they had never been so well off! Now, at last, they said, it is possible to have a few of the good things of life, if only once in a while. Eggs are available at fifteen cents each, oranges at thirty cents apiece. There may not be much for a man on a salary of sixty dollars a month; but he can have more than he ever had before.

Which is only to say that everything is relative. We cannot compare the Soviet standard of living with the standard we know in North America. In the past forty years the Soviet people have come through a terrible history—war, revolution, devastation without parallel in our time. And on top of this they have accomplished an industrial revolution that compressed into that short space of time our industrial development of more than a hundred years.

Only now are these hard-pressed people beginning to emerge into the sunlight, to raise themselves up from the ground and learn to stand, to eat, to dress and think like human beings. And, of course, like human beings everywhere, they have the same desires, the same aspirations we do. They want to share our standard of living and our ideas. The time for this is not yet. But it will come.

It is important to understand that Russia is still in a very early stage of its development. Nothing in Russia can be judged against a background like ours; we are not contemporaries. They have cut themselves off from our background and are beginning all over again, right from the start. They are going to have to learn each painful step on the road to civilization themselves, without anyone to help them. They are going to make mistakes and learn from their own errors. They will probably succeed.

Russia may have a long and brilliant future—no doubt very different from its present, though possibly retaining its basic Communist ethic as part of its tradition. But it will change its appearance with each succeeding stage of its development, in decades and centuries to come. Now it is too soon to judge Soviet civilization—it is still in its Dark Age. Russia today is often compared with Rome. If that is true, it is Rome just after the overthrow of the early kings, even before the Republic arose, before Cato and Vergil and Brutus, before Caesar and the Empire. It is still a lonely camp-fire on an Etruscan hillside, blazing eerily in the dark.

Russia is a country in transition, moving from the most primitive level of existence into a highly technical era. The Communist leaders are trying to accomplish this transition by a forced march. That is the meaning of the Seven-Year Plan. The aim is to outproduce the non-Communist world, not only in total output, but also in per capita production. This Premier Khrushchov hopes to do in steel by 1965, and in most other basic products by 1972. The plan has been called by *Izvestia* "a plan to shake the world".

Can they do it? At any rate, this is something a Communist government is peculiarly fitted to attempt. By holding down the standard of living of its own workers, by concentrating all its energies and resources on certain specific goals, by giving total direction to its brain-power, it may surpass the free world in any chosen field—in missiles, in heavy industry, in plants for export to under-developed countries.

To this end everything must be sacrificed—wages, housing, consumer goods, luxuries, pleasures, individual freedoms. There can be no personal goals. A nice house and kitchen will keep the Soviet woman at home, and this the State cannot afford. If industry is to expand at the fantastic rate they wish, every woman must work.

The only catch is how long the Soviet people will endure it. There is ample evidence that they are getting tired of this kind of sacrifice. Even the press carries letters of complaint from readers about the quality and scarcity of shoes, lipsticks, and refrigerators. (The fact that these complaints are printed at all reflects official concern with the state of public opinion.) "Life," I was sometimes told, "is just not worth living."

Yet they will probably go through with it. They have been told, and in part believe, that this sacrifice is necessary in order to build up the country for the sake of future generations. And there is still a wishful, nagging hope that the original promises of Communism will be fulfilled, that the dictatorship of the proletariat will deliver the highest possible standard of living to the greatest possible number of people.

To the West, the emergence of this new, totally directed industrial State poses several major challenges. First of all, there is the military challenge. Many people prefer to ignore this entirely, on the grounds that total war is unthinkable in the hydrogen age, and therefore no one would be foolhardy enough to start it. This, I submit, is an over-simplification of nuclear and missile strategy.

From the moment that the Soviet ICBM is in mass production —and that may be any time—we must expect the political climate of the world to change. Because from that moment on, it will not be possible to contain Communist expansion in any outlying area of the world—in the Formosa Strait, in the Middle East, or in Berlin—by relying on the atomic deterrent.

Once the Soviet intercontinental missiles, to the number of several thousand, are mounted on their launching pads, each aimed in a trajectory that will bring it down on one of the industrial or military targets of Western Europe or North America—with an accuracy that can no longer be doubted since their remarkable success in putting *sputniks* into orbit—from that moment on, the atomic deterrent has lost its value.

No Western prime minister or president will be free to say, in the face of localized Communist aggression: "Thus far and no further, or we will resort to atomic defense," since such a threat alone might carry with it the possibility of a push-button retaliation that would kill fifty million people in a quarter of an hour.

One hopes, it is true, that the Soviet leaders would not be so mad as to push the button; but equally, no democratically elected leader could take the risk of making such a threat. Consequently, the atomic deterrent will be neutralized, at least for the forseeable future, by the power and accuracy of the ICBM.

This means that local Communist aggression—and examples of it are likely to increase in frequency and intensity as the Soviet position of power grows—will have to be met on the scene with conventional weapons. Here again, the West is at a serious disadvantage. It is no secret that the Communist world has far more powerful forces, armed with conventional weapons, to bring to bear in any local conflict, than have the Western powers.

This weakness in conventional arms, in guns, tanks, planes and men, is what made the Formosa crisis of 1958 and the Berlin crisis of 1959 so treacherous, since the Western nations could only be defended against massive Communist aggression by resort to threats of nuclear deterrents, a policy now wellnigh suicidal.

How has this situation come about? Because, in the years since World War II, the people of the West have ploughed their wealth and their resources into the production of luxuries, reducing expenditure on conventional arms and relying on the "atomic shield" to protect them. Now that this shield has been shattered, the days of cheap security may be drawing to an end.

There is, however, another long-range challenge in the Soviet Seven-Year Plan. From 1955 to 1957 Soviet aid to under-developed nations, in terms of credits, loans, grants and technical assistance, amounted to $1 billion. U.S. aid for the same period was $1.2 billion.

There are now several thousand Soviet scientists, engineers and agronomists in the under-developed countries, at work building the atomic-power stations, the agricultural-experiment stations, and the irrigation dams that are urgently required for economic development. These countries are just verging on their own industrial revolutions and, in the absence of large-scale Western assistance, must begin to look to Soviet models for guidance. For example, Indonesia has a "guided democracy", Syria a "progressive directed economy".

The aim in all this is clear; it is to bring under-developed countries into the Soviet bloc, economically first, politically later. And it is also clear how much we depend on these nations for our own survival, as we have always depended on the vast areas of Africa, the Middle East, and the Far East for our sources of raw materials and markets for manufactured goods.

If ever we should lose these areas entirely to the Communist bloc—as we are losing them one by one; the trend is unmistakable—surely we would expect our own standard of living to fall, with all the political, social and economic chaos that would mean. Such is the shape of the challenge.

But, of course, it is not going to happen, because we are not going to let it happen. The great question before our generation is what we want to do about it. Do we want to organize our society, not necessarily along Soviet lines but at least along competitive lines, in order to direct our resources, in materials, technology, and brains, where they are most needed?

Are we prepared to organize our educational system, for

example? Our answer to this question must be based on certain facts. The facts in Soviet education may be summarized as follows: State subsidization, scientific specialization, and new economic incentives. Every Soviet child has an equal opportunity for education; he receives tuition free, his books free, his lodging free, and, when going to college, a salary in conformity with his marks.

Soviet education is also highly selective, in order to produce the kind of graduates that are most needed by the State. While resident college enrollment in the Soviet Union (7 per 1,000 population) is less than half the figure for Canadian-American students (17 per 1,000 population), the ratio in engineering, for example, is two to one in favour of the Soviets.

Further, in the Soviet Union every trained graduate is under an obligation to work in a designated capacity after graduation. The harshness of this regimentation is mitigated, however, by the steep rise in incentive pay for those in specialist categories. Many Soviet scientists, technical experts, and university professors earn salaries far higher than their opposite numbers in the West—a contrast all the the more noticeable in a society where the average standard of living is so low.

It may be said, therefore, that the primary goal of Soviet education is to supply the State with the personnel required to implement its programme—not to fulfil the personality needs of the individual. This does not make it any the less dangerous in the hands of a messianic dictatorship.

The vast difference in utilization of our own educational system is apparent from recent studies in this field. In a test group of Canadian Grade-12 students, who had an average of 70 or above, 1,746 went on to university, 1,423 did not. Furthermore, in a test group of university students, 1,746 had a Grade-12 average of 70 or higher and 1,535 had an average below that point. Which would seem to indicate that nearly half of our best brains are not receiving higher education at all, while nearly half the product of our universities is of inferior quality.

"If," says this study, "we could ignore a multitude of considerations and assign students at will, it would appear possible to improve the university group considerably by excluding the latter 1,535 and replacing them with the 1,423 who had an average of 70 or higher but did not go to university." (Atkinson study of *Utilization of Student Resources*, Report No. 2, University of Toronto, 1957)

We have to decide which methods we will use to mobilize the best brains and abilities of our people, to bring them forward and to ensure that they play the most useful possible role in our society. Nothing short of conscription might induce all students with high marks to go to university. To exclude the other half with low marks would also require powers of a sweeping nature. Even if those described as unpromising were not interfered with, however, it might be well to offer inducements and provide adequate facilities for those with good prospects.

The question "what are we to do?" presents itself in another, even more vital form. Are we prepared to deflect any of our resources away from the production of luxuries and toward the development of backward areas of the world? This is not to say that nothing has been done by the West to date. What has been done, however, is commensurate neither with the need nor with our resources.

Since World War II, the United States has spent an immense sum ($65 billion) on foreign aid—NATO, SEATO, Marshall Plan, and others. But only a tiny fraction (approximately $13 billion) has gone to the under-developed nations, and of this one-third was devoted to military areas—Formosa, South Korea, Turkey, etc., with a total of 200 million people. For the rest of Asia, with a total of one billion people, little was left.

Canada, along with the rest of the Commonwealth, has supplied equipment and technical assistance to under-developed areas—$3½ billion from 1950 to 1958. Canada's contribution to date, however, is less than one-quarter of one per cent of our national income. The conclusion is inescapable that the "have"

nations are concentrating their wealth on their own development and letting the devil take the hindmost.

A British economist, Barbara Ward, has suggested that if the
wealthier nations contributed only one per cent of their national
incomes to world development, the total would easily cover all
the need. Initially, this would mean higher taxes, and fewer
TV sets, dishwashers, and blue mink coats for most of us. It
would, however, not mean less work—indeed it would solve
our unemployment problems for a long time to come.

After all, the Soviet Government is not supplying its people
with these things (there are less than six million TV sets in the
Soviet Union), *and* putting on a $1 billion development scheme
for the under-developed nations of Asia. This factor may, indeed, go a long way toward explaining the low standard of living
we have noted in the Soviet Union.

It is this failure of the democratic world to take thought for
the morrow that lends colour to the Communist tenet of faith
that capitalism will destroy itself. This is what Premier Khrushchov means when he tells Vice President Nixon that the latter's grandchildren will live under Communism, or when he
tells the West rhetorically: "We will bury you."

It was, indeed, naïve to think that the hard-headed disciple
of Marxism-Leninism would change his mind on the future of
capitalism when he saw America. Those who watched his
progress across the United States, going through department
stores, or looking over supermarkets, may have nodded their
heads with the pious hope that it would "show the old so-and-
so". But what did it show him? That we are spending our
wealth on today, while he believes he is spending his on tomorrow?

All these questions, therefore, resolve themselves into one:
are we prepared to defend the things we value most, which are,
presumably, our security and our way of life? For these are the
things that are in danger—our security from the military threat,
our way of life from the economic threat to our standard of
living.

We have the courage, certainly, as we have always had, to defend our civilization in moments of great peril. We have the means, for we are still far richer in material resources, skills and tools than the Communist world. We *can* do it. But will we?

Something like this, I submit—a redirection of our material and spiritual values—can happen in a democratic society only if the people themselves demand it, either through foresight or through fear. It is vain to look for leaders. Under responsible government, the leaders give the people what they think the people want. Such is the glory—and in time of crisis the weakness—of democracy. The people must lead, the leaders will follow. But the people can lead only if they themselves are well informed and well advised.

Returning to Canada after nine thousand miles of travel inside the Soviet Union is like returning to the light of day. Never before has our life in all its fullness seemed to me so bright, promising, rich, various, and worth while. I do not think for a moment that we will allow this great inheritance to slip from us.

I have every confidence in the wisdom and ability of our people. Already, as a result of the astounding developments in Soviet science, there is discernible in our society a trend away from the unrestricted pursuit of luxury, as in the past, toward an era of greater responsibility—responsibility to ourselves, to our children and to all mankind. And if the *sputniks* awakened us to that and nothing else, we could be forever grateful.

The prospect before the democratic world is dark and uncertain. But optimism is never out of place, provided it is based on facts as they are and not on illusion. I should like to leave this page with the words of a great optimist, Robert Browning—the last words he ever wrote. He was one, he said, who

> *Never dreamed, though right were worsted,*
> *wrong would triumph,*
> *Held we fall to rise, are baffled to fight better,*
> *Sleep to wake.*

INDEX

914.7